BOOK
—OF—
DATES

A CHRONOLOGY OF
WORLD HISTORY

GUY ARNOLD

RAINBOW
·BOOKS·

The publishers wish to thank the following for supplying photographs for this book:

19 M. Holford; 29 S. Halliday; 33 M. Holford; 35 Giraudon; 36 *(top right)* Mansell Collection; 38 *(bottom)* Bibliothèque Nationale, Paris; 39 *(top)* Fotomas; 39 *(bottom)* Scala, Milan; 46 Mary Evans Picture Library; 48 *(bottom right)* Service de Documentation, Paris; 49 Mary Evans Picture Library; 59 Musée de la Ville de Strasbourg; 61 Mansell Collection; 63 Kodak Museum; 65 *(bottom right)* National Portrait Gallery; 71 ZEFA; 72 *(right)* Mansel Collection; 73 Science Museum; 74 BBC Hulton Picture Library; 85 *(bottom right)* Atomic Energy Commission.

This edition published in 1993 by Rainbow Books,
Elsley House, 24–30 Great Titchfield Street, London W1P 7AD
Originally published in 1988 by Kingfisher Books.
The date charts were first published in 1983 by Kingfisher
Books in *Datelines of World History*.

10 9 8 7 6 5 4 3 2 1

ISBN 1 85698 031 6

Editor: John Grisewood
Assistant editor: Nicola Barber
Designer: Ben White
Cover illustration: Ian Jackson

Printed in Spain

CONTENTS

CIVILIZATIONS

the coloured bands represent the time span and rise and fall of each empire where appropriate

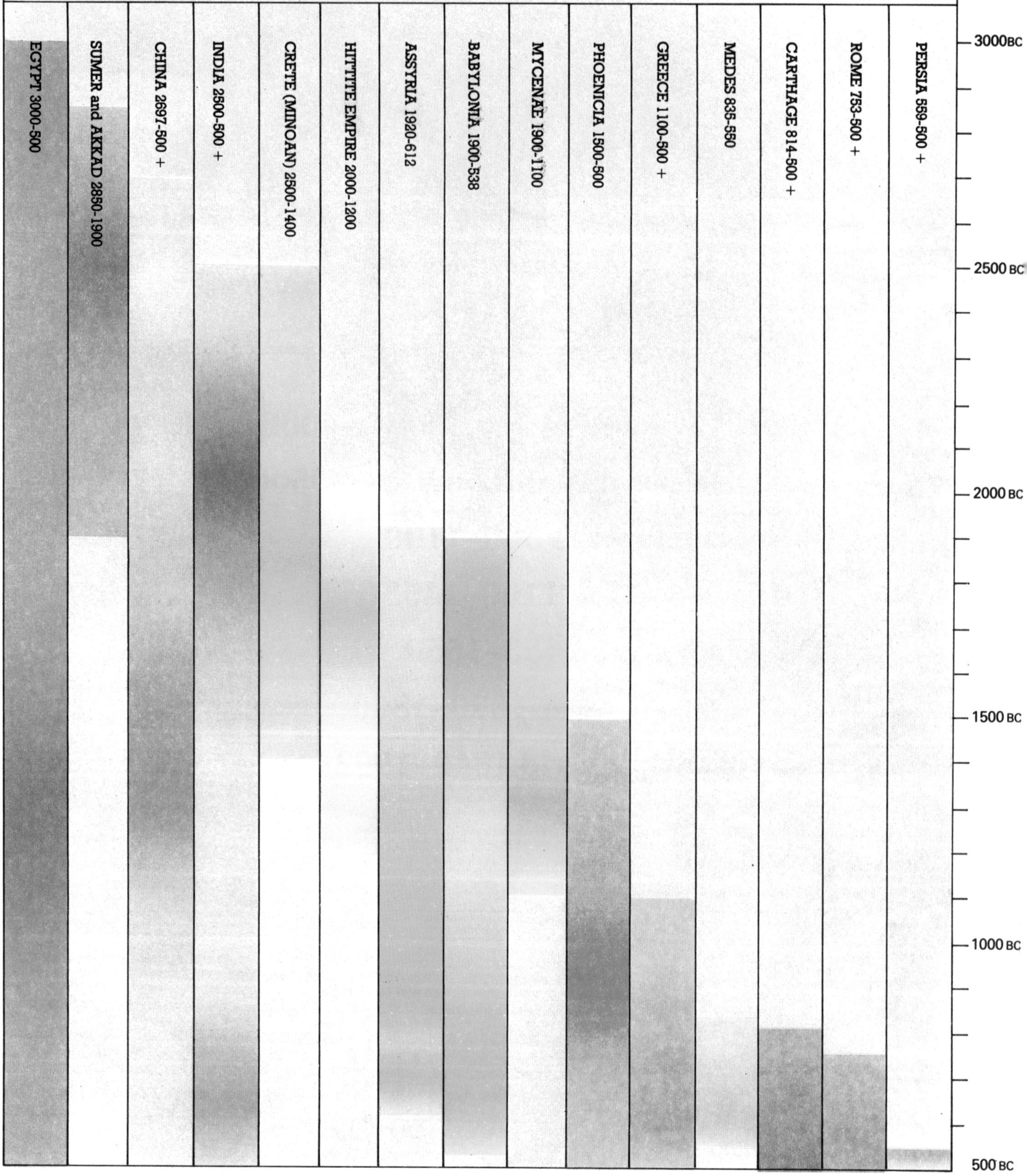

EGYPT 3000-500

SUMER and AKKAD 2850-1900

CHINA 2697-500 +

INDIA 2500-500 +

CRETE (MINOAN) 2500-1400

HITTITE EMPIRE 2000-1200

ASSYRIA 1920-612

BABYLONIA 1900-538

MYCENAE 1900-1100

PHOENICIA 1500-500

GREECE 1100-500 +

MEDES 835-550

CARTHAGE 814-500 +

ROME 753-500 +

PERSIA 559-500 +

- 3000 BC
- 2500 BC
- 2000 BC
- 1500 BC
- 1000 BC
- 500 BC

EARLY CIVILIZATIONS

The first great civilizations grew up along river valleys: Egypt on the Nile, Sumer between the Euphrates and Tigris; in China a civilization appeared on the banks of the Yellow River and in India along the Indus. But the Fertile Crescent which stretches from Egypt in North Africa to the Gulf was the cradle of civilizations – Egypt, Babylon, Sumer, Assyria.

40,000BC –500BC

An Assyrian king watches prisoners-of-war dragging a huge statue of a winged human-headed bull from the stone quarries.

MOVEMENT

40,000–29,000 Cro-Magnon people move into Europe from Asia.
30,000–20,000 Humans appear in Australia.
30,000–10,000 Early (Neanderthal) humans replaced by hunters in Africa.

28,000 *Homo sapiens* cross land bridge from Asia to North America.
16,000–10,000 Hunters roam southern Europe.
10,000 Hunters reach tip of South America and south Africa.
6000 First settlements in Crete.
2300 Semites from Arabia migrate to Mesopotamia to found Assyrian and Babylonian empires.
2200 Greeks arrive in Crete.
2150 Aryans invade Indus Valley.
2100 Abraham migrates from Ur.
2000 Beginnings of great migrations east and south from west Africa. Hittites move into Anatolia (modern Turkey).
1300 Medes and Persians move into Iran.
1200 Devastation through Asia Minor, Near East, Greek world by Sea People.
1100–1050 Dorian invasions of Greece.
500 Bantu peoples spreading in east Africa.

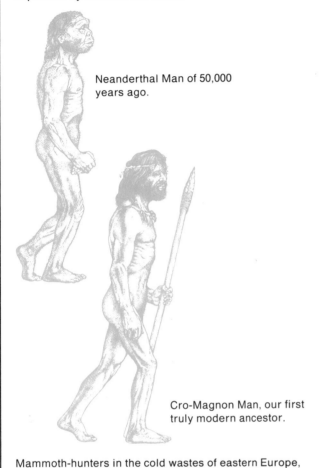

Neanderthal Man of 50,000 years ago.

Cro-Magnon Man, our first truly modern ancestor.

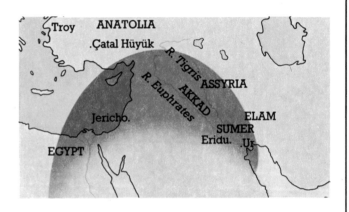

The Fertile Crescent, the area where western civilization developed along the river banks.

Mammoth-hunters in the cold wastes of eastern Europe, 25,000 years ago.

TECHNOLOGY

10,000 Development of hunting weapons at the end of the Ice Age.
8000 Development of agriculture – farming and settled villages in eastern Anatolia.
7000 Metal working in Anatolia.
Walled settlement at Jericho.
6000 Cattle raising in Anatolia. Early trade in obsidian and flint. Çatal Hüyük – one of first towns.
6000–5000 Neolithic period begins.
5000 Village farm communities along Hwang-ho River in China.

Pebbles and flints were chipped to make the first tools.

5000–2000 Farming spreads south in Africa.
4500 Real metal work begins – heating and pouring metal.
4000 Wheel in Mesopotamia. Use of potter's wheel. Yang-shao rice farming culture in China.
3500 Copper tools in Thailand.
3100 Early use of bronze in Egypt and Sumer
3000 Cities and temples in Sumer and Egypt – use of bricks for building.
Windmill culture in Britain.
Agriculture in Tehuacan Valley, Mexico.
3000–2000 Bronze Age in Anatolia.
Stone villages in Crete.
2500 Bronze tools in Thailand.
Metal working reaches Indus Valley.
2000 Bronze age begins in Europe.
1600 Mycenaeans trade through Mediterranean.
1500 Bronze worked in Anyang region of China.
1400 Iron Age reaches western Asia/India.
1200 Horses and chariots used on Sahara trade routes.
1000 Iron tools in Ganges Valley.

CULTURE

25,000 Hunters make clay models.
20,000 Early cave paintings in France and Spain.
6000–5000 Africa rock paintings.

Hieroglyphs – the ancient Egyptian form of writing.

4236 First date in Egyptian calendar.
3760 First date in Jewish calendar.
3372 First date in Mayan calendar.
3100 Sumerians devise first known system of writing.
3000 First pottery in Mexico.
2780 First pyramid in Egypt.
2200 Linear (A) Minoan writing.
Linear (B) Greek writing.
1379 Amenhotep inaugurates sun worship in Egypt.
1300 Construction of temples at Abu Simbel.
1200–1028 Twelve tribes adopt Yahweh worship in Israel.
1100 First Chinese dictionary.
1000 Phoenicians in Tyre employ full alphabet.
Rig Vega (religious text) compiled in India.
800 Homeric poems, *Iliad* and *Odyssey*, take their final shape.
776 First Olympic Games.
621 Dracon – laws for Athens.
594 Solon – news laws for Athens.
580 Nebuchadnezzar constructs the Hanging Gardens of Babylon.
563 Birth of Siddhartha Gautama (The Buddha).
551 Birth of Kung Fu-tzu (Confucius).
508 Cleisthenes introduces democracy in Athens.

EARLY CIVILIZATIONS 40,000BC–2000BC

THE FERTILE CRESCENT

8000 Eastern Anatolia (Turkey): Farming and settled villages.
Domestication of sheep and cattle.
7000 Anatolia: Metal working in copper, silver, gold.
Jericho (Israel): Walled settlements.
6000–5000 Çatal Hüyük (Anatolia): one of the world's first towns – perhaps 5000 population.
5000 Sumer: First agricultural settlements in river valleys of Tigris and Euphrates.
4500 Egypt and Sumer: Real metal work begins – heating and pouring metal.
4000–3500 Mesopotamia: Potter's wheel first used. Disastrous floods.
Sumer: First towns – Ur, Eridu.
Egypt: White painted pottery. Ships in Mediterranean.
3100 Egypt: First Egyptian dynasty. First harps and flutes.
Sumer: First known system of writing using 2000 pictographic signs – on clay tablets. Early use of bronze.
3000 Elamite civilization in Iran.
Sumer and Egypt: Cities and temples built. Bricks used for building.
Sumerians grow barley – make bread and beer. Invention of wheel.
Phoenicians settle eastern Mediterranean (Levant).
3000–2400 Troy – the first city state.
3000–2000 Bronze Age in Fertile Crescent.
First iron objects made in Mesopotamia 3000–2500.
2800–2400 City states of Sumer at their zenith – Sumer the world's richest market. Metal coins replace barley as legal tender.
2800–2175 Old Kingdom in Egypt.
2780 First pyramid in Egypt at Saqqara. Designed by Imhotep.
2772 Egypt introduces a 365-day calendar.
2750 Gilgamesh, legendary king of Uruk, Sumeria.
2700 Cheops rules Egypt and builds the Great Pyramid at Giza.
2500 First Egyptian mummies.
2450–2270 Akkadian empire – the largest to date.
2350 Sargon, the Akkadian emperor, conquers Sumer.
2300 Semites from Arabia migrate to Mesopotamia to found the Assyrian and Babylonian empires.
2230 Fall of Akkadian empire.
2140–2030 Empire of Ur reaches to Perian Gulf – a thriving commerce.
2133 Middle Kingdom in Egypt: the 7th dynasty.
2100 Abraham migrates from Ur.
2030 Decline of Sumer.

THE REST OF THE WORLD

30,000 Neanderthal humans still exist in Cyrenaica, N. Africa.
30,000–10,000 Human hunters in Africa.
16,000–10,000 Hunters roam southern Europe – animal paintings at Lascaux in France and Altamira in Spain.
15,000–10,000 Africa cooler than today – last rainy period in north.
10,000 End of Ice Age. Hunting weapons develop – disappearance of large mammals.
8400 First domesticated dog – Idaho (North America).
6000–5000 African rock paintings.
6000 New Stone Age.
6000–5000 Earliest settlements in Crete.
5000 Sea separates Britain from Europe.
China: Village farming communities along the Yellow River.
5000 Neolithic Africa: working of polished stone; development of civilizations at Fayoum and Nubia in Nile Valley.
5000–2000 Agriculture spreads southwards in Africa.
4000–3000 Coloured pottery from Russia reaches China. Cretan ships in Mediterranean.
3500 Thailand: Copper tools.
3372 First date in Mayan calendar.
3100 Early use of bronze.
3000 Wild horses domesticated in the Ukraine.
3000 Development of agriculture in Tehuacan Valley, Mexico – maize, beans, squash.
Villages and towns on the coast of Peru.
First pottery in Mexico.
3000–2000 Crete trades with Egypt, Levant, Anatolia.
Weaving loom in Europe
2697 Huang-ti, emperor of China.
Metal working reaches the Indus Valley – start of major civilization there.
2500 Early Minoan civilization – the foundation of Knossos, Crete.
First picture of skiing – rock carving, Rodoy, S. Norway.
Metal working spreads through Europe.
2350 China: Yao dynasty.
2250 Yu-shun, emperor of China.
China: Hsia dynasty.
2200 Greek speakers arrive in Crete: Linear (A) – Minoan writing (still undeciphered): Linear (B) – early Greek writing (deciphered in 1952).
2150 Aryans first invade Indus Valley.
2000 Beginnings of Bantu migrations from west Africa eastwards and southwards.
Cotton is cultivated in Peru.

EARLY TECHNOLOGY

A two-wheeled cart of about 2000BC. The first wheels were probably a section of log with a hole for an axle.

SETTLED AGRICULTURE

When our early ancestors settled to farm instead of roving to hunt the first civilizations became possible. Growing crops and domesticating animals in one place changed the pattern of human behaviour. Populations became larger and produced more food than their immediate needs. This allowed some people to be specialists – craftsmen, artists, builders or administrators – instead of everyone having to gather food or hunt. They could barter the surplus and this was the beginning of trade. The growth of cities followed.

People begin to sow seeds in prepared ground in about 8600BC.

Primitive irrigation – the *shaduf,* of about 5000BC.

A Russian hut built of mammoth bones 25,000 years ago. Where timber was scarce hunters made do with bones.

The first apemen of 1.4 million years ago used fire for warmth and to ward off wild animals.

Cave people cooking meat over a fire, 25,000BC.

A coracle of about 600BC from Wales. It was made of animal skins fixed to a wooden frame. Coracles are still used in Wales though canvas and tar have replaced the skins.

Copper and tin being smelted in a charcoal fire, 3000BC. The bellows are used to raise the heat to separate the metal from its ore.

A dugout canoe, 600BC. This is one of the very earliest forms of water transport.

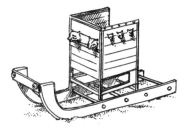

A sled used by the Babylonians in about 200BC. The first sleds date back as far as 5800BC.

ANCIENT EGYPT

An Egyptian lavatory. People continued to use 'earth closets' and chamber pots until the end of the 17th century AD!

Egyptian tomb painting, 1600BC. The Egyptians painted people with two left feet – you can only see the big toes!

Bread being baked in an Egyptian oven, 2000BC.

The Egyptians developed the equal arm balance to weigh grain about 7000 years ago.

An Egyptian gondola of 1375BC. As most rich people lived along the Nile travel by boat was common.

EGYPTIAN POWER

1786–1567 Dynasties 13 to 17: period of the Hyksos invaders who found the 15th dynasty.
1567–1087 New Kingdom.
1504–1450 Period of expansion under Thutmosis III – controls Palestine, Syria, and south to Nubia.
1500 Egypt is the world's greatest power.
1479 Battle of Megiddo – Thutmosis III conquers Palestine.
1420–1379 Amenhotep III – the Golden Age of Egypt.
1379 Amenhotep IV starts sun worship and takes name Akhenaton – other gods abolished.
1361 Pharaoh Tutankhamun – idea of single god abandoned – return to old gods.
1320 Rameses I founds 19th dynasty.
1292–1225 Rameses II (the Great) – restoration of Egypt's Asiatic empire.
1290 Battle of Qadesh against Hittites – both sides claim victory.
1283 Peace between Egypt and the Hittites.
1280 Construction of temples at Abu Simbel.
1250 Moses leads Israelites out of Egypt.
1232 Israelites in Canaan are defeated by Egyptians under Merneptah, son of Rameses II.
1200–1167 Rameses III.
1200–1087 20th dynasty.
1179 Egypt invaded by the Confederation of Sea Peoples – Philistines, Greeks, Sardinians, Sicilians; defeated by Rameses III.
1087–751 High priests of Amun become rulers of Egypt.

AEGEAN WORLD

2000 Bronze Age begins in Europe.
Earliest Minoan palace at Knossos.
2000–1450 Minoan Crete dominates Aegean.
1900–1600 Development of Mycenaean culture.
1650–1450 Growth of Mycenaean power centred on Mycenae and Pylos.
1600 Mycenaeans trade throughout the Mediterranean.
1500 Minoans face growing competition from Mycenae.
1450–1400 Collapse of Minoan power.
1400 Knossos, the Minoan capital, is destroyed by fire. Mycenaeans occupy Crete.
1300 Arcadians settling in central Peloponnese.
1200 Aegean devastated by Sea People.
1193 Destruction of Troy by Greeks.
1150–1100 Collapse of Mycenaean power.
1100 Dorians invade Greece from north, destroying the Mycenaean citadels.
1045 Death of Codron – last king of Athens.
1000 Greeks establish colonies in Aegean.

THE EAST

2000 Hittites move into Anatolia. Hittites monopolize the secret of working iron.
2000–1225 Patriarchs of Genesis (Bible).
1950 End of Ur empire.
1925 Hittites conquer Babylon.
1920–1850 Assyrian merchants establish a colony at Cappadocia in Anatolia.
1900–1600 Amorites at Babylon.
1830 Founding of first Babylonian dynasty.
1830–1810 Assyria under Babylonian rule.
1810 King Shamshi-Adad makes Assyria independent.
1800 Accession of Hammurabi of Babylon, author of great Code of Laws.
1800–1750 Babylon conquers the city states of northern and southern Mesopotamia.
1750–1500 Old Kingdom of the Hittites.
1700 Expansion of Hittites across Anatolia into Syria.
1600 Hittites take Aleppo.
1500 Hittite royal succession becomes hereditary; Hittites control all Anatolia.
Indus Valley civilization falls to Aryan invasion: destruction of Mohenjo-Daro.
China: First historical period begins under the Shang dynasty; Anyang becomes capital. Bronze is worked in Anyang region.
1500–1000 India: Early period in Ganges Valley.
1430–1200 New Kingdom of Hittites.
1400 Iron Age reaches western Asia.
1390–1350 Suppiluliumas, greatest Hittite king, reconquers Anatolia, subjects northern Syria and makes the Mitanni tribes into Hittite subjects.
1366 Assurubalit I of Assyria – period of expansion.
1300 Medes and Persians move into Iran.
1232–1116 Decline then new growth of Assyria.
1200 Sea People invade Anatolia – Hittites disappear from history except in Syria.
1170 Growing power of Phoenicians in Levant – Tyre is main city.
1146–1123 Nebuchadnezzar I defeats Elamites but is routed by Assyrians.
1140 Phoenicians found Utica, their first N. African colony.
1125 Nebuchadnezzar beats back Assyrian invasion of Babylon.
1116 Tiglath-pileser I of Assyria conquers Babylon and controls Asian trade.
1100–900 Aramaic tribes invade Babylonia.
First Chinese dictionary.
1093–939 Assyria just survives as a power.
1050 Philistines conquer Israel.
1027 China: Emperor Wu Wang founds Chou dynasty and establishes feudal system by overthrowing Shang dynasty.
1020 Samuel, last of Judges, anoints Saul king of the Israelites. They rebel against Philistines.
1000 Death of Saul at Gilboa. David, king of Judah, and then Israel – makes Jerusalem his capital.
India: Iron tools are made in Ganges Valley.
Rig Vega (sacred hymns) compiled.

MEDITERRANEAN

1000–700 Etruscans in upper Italy – race with a unique language and religion.
814 Phoenicians found Carthage.
800 Homer composes the *Iliad* and *Odyssey* at about this time.
776 First Olympic Games in Greece.
753 Foundation of Rome.
700–500 Formation of Greek city states.
683 Athens replaces hereditary kings with nine archons chosen annually from the nobles.
650–500 Self-made, one man rule (tyranny) in Greek cities.
621 Dracon proves Athens with its first written laws which are severe.
600–480 Growth and expansion of Carthage.
594 Solon made sole archon of Athens. New laws replace those of Dracon.
510 Rebellion at Rome – Tarquinius Superbus, the last king of Rome overthrown.
509 Foundation of Roman republic.
508 Cleisthenes introduces democracy in Athens. Rome survives attack by Lars Porsena of Clusium – Horatio holds the bridge!
Treaty between Rome and Carthage gives Latium to Rome and Africa to Carthage.
507 Sparta attempts to restore the aristocracy in Athens – the beginning of a century of rivalry.

GREAT EMPIRES

1000–774 Great period of Tyre under Phoenicians.
973–933 Solomon – development of trade, laws, taxes; great buildings – temple at Jerusalem.
933 Solomon's kingdom is divided between his sons – Israel (the north) under Jeroboam; and Judah (the south) under Rehoboam.
933–586 Judah.
933–722 Israel.
900–625 Assyria and Babylon constantly at war.
748–727 Tiglath-pileser III – huge Assyrian expansion to include Israel, Damascus, Babylon.
722 Sargon of Assyria captures Samaria and brings an end to the kingdom of Israel.
701 Nineveh is made Assyrian captial.
689 After revolt the Assyrians destroy Babylon.
625–538 Neo-Babylonian empire.
612 Babylonians, Medes and Scythians destroy Nineveh.
609 End of Assyrian empire.
605–561 Nebuchadnezzar II of Babylon defeats Egyptians at Carchemish – brings Judah under Babylon.
586 Nebuchadnezzar retakes Jerusalem, sacks it – people of Judah taken captive to Babylon.
559–530 Cyrus the Great founds the Persian empire.
550 Media incorporated into the Persian empire.
546 Battle of Sardis – Cyrus defeats Croesus of Lydia.
539 Babylon, Phoenicia and Judah come under Persia.
530 Death of Cyrus – the Persian empire includes all Asia Minor, Babylonia, Syria and Palestine.
525 Egypt brought under Persia (until 404BC).
521–486 Darius rules Persian empire.

DEVELOPMENTS

1200–800 India: Aryans worship nature gods.
1000–950 China: Western Chou dynasty establishes its capital at Hao in Wei Valley.
800–550 India: Aryan expansion. Gradual development of caste system.
770–256 China: Eastern Chou dynasty.
722–481 China: Period of loose confederations under the Eastern Chou dynasty.
600 India: Early cities in Ganges Valley.
563 India: Birth of Siddhartha Gautama who became the Buddha (the Enlightened One).
551 China: Birth of Kung Fu-tzu (Confucius), died 497BC.
500 Bantu peoples spreading in east Africa.

THE ASSYRIANS

The Assyrians dominated the Fertile Crescent for 600 years from 120 to 600BC. At their most powerful they controlled Syria, Palestine, Phoenicia and northern Egypt. They were great builders and levied heavy taxes on their subject peoples. Their army was the best trained the ancient world had yet seen.

THE HEBREWS

Traditionally Abraham led the Hebrews out of Ur but it was king David (died 973BC) who established a Hebrew Kingdom with its capital at Jerusalem. His son Solomon built the temple and walls of Jerusalem but under his sons the kingdom split into Israel and Judah. Judaism was the first religion to establish the idea of only one God.

THE CLASSICAL WORLD

The Classical period saw the foundations of our era. In the West the Greeks and Romans left us ideas about government and law, philosophy and art which are still part of our everyday lives; in the east the Chin dynasty united China and built the Great Wall. Three of the world's great religions – Christianity, Hinduism and Confucianism – grew and flourished at this time.

500BC–AD500

A procession winding its way to the Temple of Apollo at Delphi, Greece.

THE CLASSICAL WORLD 500BC–AD500

THE WEST

500 Etruscan empire at its most powerful.
480 Greek naval victory at Salamis.
477–405 Golden Age of Athens.
450–400 Etruscan empire in decline.
356–338 Philip II of Macedon unites Greek states.
336–323 Alexander the Great conquers Persian empire.
264–241 Rome wins the First Punic War against Carthage.
218–201 Second Punic War – Hannibal crosses the Alps. Scipio annihilates Carthaginian army. Rome at war with Macedon – Rome gains Greece.
149–146 Third Punic War – destruction of Carthage.
60 Triumvirate of Caesar, Pompey and Crassus to rule Rome.
44 Assassination of Caesar.
31 Battle of Actium – Octavian (later Augustus) defeats Antony.
23BC–AD14 Augustus (Princeps) makes himself first emperor of Rome.
AD43 Romans invade Britain.
AD68 Death of Nero. Year of the Four Emperors.
AD70 Titus captures Jerusalem. *Diaspora* (dispersal) of Jews.
AD98–117 Trajan – last period of Roman expansion.
180 Death of Marcus Aurelius. End of Golden Age of Rome.
268 Goths sack Athens, Sparta, Corinth.
286 Diocletian divides the Roman empire into west and east.
313 Emperor Constantine the Great issues Edict of Toleration (for Christianity) at Milan.
330 Constantine founds Constantinople.

The Romans were superb civil engineers. They built aqueducts to carry water over huge distances to supply cities and irrigate fields.

379–395 Theodosius the Great, emperor of the east.
385?–407 Legions leave Britain.
410 Alaric and the Goths sack Rome.
451 Attila and the Huns invade Gaul.
476 Romulus Augustus the last emperor of Rome deposed – end of western empire.

THE EAST & AFRICA

550–530 Achaemenid empire in Persia.
500 Nok culture in N. Nigeria.
500BC–AD320 Kushite kingdom centred on Meröe, Sudan.
458–424 Partition of China by Han, Chao and Wei.
403–221 Period of warring states in China.
321–184 Mauryan dynasty. Capital at Pataliputra, N.E. India.
221–207 Ch'in dynasty unites China.
214 Building of the Great Wall.
202BC–AD9 Han dynasty in China.
184–72BC Sunga dynasty in Ganges Valley, India.
140–87BC Wu Ti – 'The Martial Emperor'. Expansion of China.
100BC–AD225 Munda kings rule the Deccan, central India.
AD43 China conquers Tonkin and Assam.
AD74–94 China brings the states of Turkestan under its control – opens silk trade to west.
78–96 Kamishka founds 2nd Kushana dynasty. Capital at Peshawar, Pakistan.
166 Presents from Roman Emperor Marcus Aurelius to Chinese Emperor Huang-ti – one of the few known direct contacts between the two empires.
200 Iron Age in central Africa.
220–264 China divided into three kingdoms.
226 Ardashir founds Sassanid empire in Persia.
313 Collapse of Chinese colonies in Korea.
317–589 Southern and Northern dynasties again divide China.
320 Axum brings Kushite empire to an end.
320–525 Gupta dynasty in north India.
361 Empress Jingo of Japan invades Korea.
407–553 First Mongol empire of Avars.

PHILOSOPHY & ART

460–429 Pericles strives to make Athens the most beautiful city in the world.
450 12 Tables of Roman Law.
Herodotus in Egypt.
429 Acropolis of Athens completed.
Birth of Plato.
399 Socrates put to death for heretical teaching.
213 Banning of books in China. Roll silk used for new writing.
191 Ban on old literature in China withdrawn; scholars transcribe into new scripts.
180 Early Meroitic writing in Africa.
155–130 Liu Teh collects archaic scripts in China; compilation of early writing, especially Taoism.
124 Philosophical teachings of Confucius become official in China.
100–1BC Period of great literary importance in China.
50BC Golden Age of Latin literature – Caesar, Virgil, Horace, Catullus and Cicero.
45BC Caesar establishes the Julian calendar.
AD18 Death of Ovid.
65 Death of Seneca.
80 Colosseum and Baths of Titus completed in Rome.
124 Pantheon completed in Rome.
150 *Geographia* of Claudius Ptolemy.

RELIGION

300 First Hindu philosophical schools start.
250 Hebrew scriptures translated into Greek – the *Septuagint*.
4?BC Birth of Christ.
AD30? Crucifixion of Christ
33–156 Taosim flourishes under the tutelage of Chang Taoling in China.
45 Paul begins missionary journeys.
58 Buddhism introduced to China.
65 St Mark's Gospel.
70 First *diaspora* (dispersal) of Jews.
St Matthew's Gospel.
75 St Luke's Gospel.
95 St John's Gospel; Revelations.
135 Final *diaspora* of Jews.
226 Zoroastrianism becomes official Persian religion under Sassanian rule.
246 Mani founds Manichaeism in Persia. Crucified by Zoroastrians in 276.
313 Edict of Toleration at Milan – Christianity allowed in Roman empire.
350 Christianity reaches Ethiopia.
354 Birth of Augustine in Numidia, N. Africa.
372 Korea receives Buddhism from China.
396 St Augustine made bishop of Hippo, N. Africa.
401–417 Pope Innocent I claims universal authority over Roman Church.
432 Mission of St Patrick to Ireland.
478 First Shinto shrines appear in Japan.

The capital of one of the many pillars put up on the orders of the Indian emperor Ashoka in the 3rd century BC.

THE GOLDEN AGE OF GREECE

For more than 2000 years the West has been influenced by developments which took place in Greece during the fifth century BC. This Golden Age saw a brief period of unity when the city states of Greece united to oppose the Persian threat under the Great Kings, Darius and Xerxes. Under Pericles Athens pioneered the idea of democracy – one man, one vote. He made Athens a city of beauty, art and culture. Dramatists such as Aeschylus, Sophocles and Euripides , sculptors like Myron, Polycleitus and Pheidias, Thucydides (the historian) and the philosophers Socrates and Plato produced ideas which have influenced us ever since. But the last 30 years of the century saw a bitter war between Athens and Sparta which permanently weakened the Greek world. The importance of the Greeks was that they asked questions: how a state should be run, what the laws ought to be and why.

THE CLASSICAL WORLD 500BC–250BC

GREEK & WORLD CULTURES

500 Africa: Appearance of iron-using.
Nok culture in northern Nigeria.
497 Death of Pythagoras, Greek philosopher and scientist (b 581).
499–494 Ionians of Anatolia, with help from Athens, rebel against Persian rule under Darius.
490 Defeat of Darius at battle of Marathon.
480 Xerxes of Persia invades Greece after battle of Thermopylae. Persian fleet defeated at Salamis, necessitating retreat of Persian army.
479 Defeat of Persian army at Plataea. Their fleet destroyed.
477–405 Golden Age of Athens.
470 Carthaginian explorer, Hanno, maps west African coast by sailing down it as far as Cameroun.
460 First Peloponnesian War between Athens and Sparta.
460 Hippocrates, Greek physician – 'The Father of Medicine'.
460–429 Pericles, leader of Athens.
450 Herodotus, the Greek historian, in Egypt.
447 Construction of Parthenon at Athens.
445 Nehemiah rebuilds walls of Jerusalem.
431–404 Second Peloponnesian War.
411 Revolution in Athens – dictatorship of Five Thousand, but democracy soon restored.
406 Athenian fleet defeats Spartans at Arginusae.
405 Spartan fleet under Lysander destroys Athenian fleet at Aegospotami.
404 Lysander captures Athens and sets up government of Thirty Tyrants.
403 Pausanias restores democracy in Athens.
395 Athens, Thebes, Argos in coalition against Sparta. Death of Lysander.
394 Battle of Coronae – Sparta defeats coalition.
384–322 Aristotle, Greek philosopher.
370–362 Thebes forms Arcadian League against Sparta, ending Spartan power.
356–336 Philip II of Macedon – controls all of Greece.
336 Assassination of Philip of Macedon.
336–323 Alexander III of Macedon, 'The Great' maintains order in Greece and creates his empire.
323 Death of Alexander. End of great age of Greece.
323 Birth of Euclid, the Greek philosopher.
288 Birth of Archimedes, Greek mathematician and inventor.
265 First Roman contact with Greek medicine, through prisoners of war.
250 Hebrew scriptures translated into Greek – the *Septuagint*.

OTHER EMPIRES

770–256 China: Eastern Chou dynasty reigns powerless at Loyang.
550–221 India: Aryan parts divided into many states.
Maghada empire established in north-east India.
500–250 Africa: Kushite kingdom centred on Meröe.
496 Romans take over Latium by defeating Latins at Lake Regillus.
494 Revolt of the debt-ridden 'plebeians' (peasant masses) – they win independence and increased rights from Roman patricians.
493 Roman-Latin alliance – the Latin League – fight the Etruscans.
480–400 Carthage develops sea power and controls the western Mediterranean and western Sicily.
465–424 Artaxerxes I rules Persia.
424–404 Darius II of Persia.
404–359 Artaxerxes II – Egypt breaks free of Persian rule.
380–343 30th Egyptian dynasty – last native house to rule the country.
390 Gauls sack Rome.
366 First plebeian council elected in Rome.
343–275 Rome comes to dominate Italy.
343 Persia retakes Egypt.
338–330 Darius III.
323 Alexander's generals divide up empire.
General Ptolemy becomes satrap (ruler) of Egypt.
321–184 India: Chandragupta founds the Mauryan dynasty.
320 Ptolemy takes Jerusalem.
312 General Seleucus takes Syria.
312 Appius Claudius builds the Appian Way from Rome to Capua, near Naples.
306 Trade treaty between Rome and Carthage.
305 Foundation of Seleucid empire and dynasty based at Babylon.
Ptolemy takes title of pharaoh in Egypt.
300 Treaty between Rome and Carthage.
300 Central America: Mayan civilization in Yucatan.
N. Korea: State of Choson.
287 Full equality between patricians and plebeians in Rome.
273–232 India: Asoka – greatest of Mauryan emperors.
264–241 First Punic War between Rome and Carthage – the beginning of a century of struggle for mastery of the Mediterranean world.
254 In Sicily, Rome takes Palermo from Carthage.

GREECE'S GOLDEN AGE

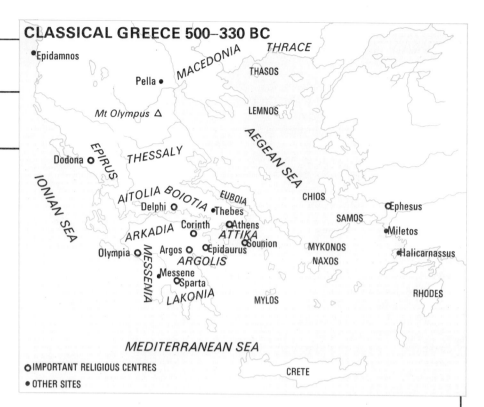

CLASSICAL GREECE 500–330 BC

- Epidamnos
- THRACE
- MACEDONIA
- THASOS
- Pella
- Mt Olympus △
- LEMNOS
- EPIRUS
- THESSALY
- Dodona
- AEGEAN SEA
- IONIAN SEA
- AITOLIA
- BOIOTIA
- EUBOIA
- CHIOS
- Delphi
- Thebes
- Ephesus
- SAMOS
- ARKADIA
- Corinth
- Athens
- Miletus
- ATTIKA
- Sounion
- MYKONOS
- Halicarnassus
- Olympia
- Argos
- Epidaurus
- NAXOS
- MESSENIA
- ARGOLIS
- Messene
- Sparta
- MYLOS
- LAKONIA
- RHODES
- MEDITERRANEAN SEA
- CRETE

○ IMPORTANT RELIGIOUS CENTRES
● OTHER SITES

THE HOME

Around the splendid public buildings of a Greek city clustered the houses of the citizens. These were made of mudbrick on a stone foundation. The average citizen lived in a house about 18 metres (60 feet) square. The ground floor rooms were grouped around a central courtyard, overlooked on three sides by the upper story. These houses were usually grouped together.

A Greek country house. It was made from unbaked bricks. The upper floor was held up by wooden beams.

The agora was the Greek market place where people from the surrounding villages brought goods to sell.

A Greek sculptor making a bronze head by the 'lost-wax' method.

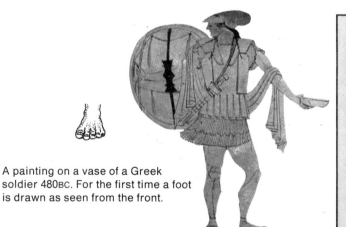

A painting on a vase of a Greek soldier 480BC. For the first time a foot is drawn as seen from the front.

ALEXANDER THE GREAT

No other leader has captured the imagination as has Alexander. He became king of Macedon in 336BC at the age of 20; by his death in 323BC he had conquered the Persian Empire and ruled from Greece to Kashmir and south to Egypt. One of the greatest soldiers of all time, he created the first European-based empire. The city of Alexandria in Egypt was his most famous monument. Alexander became 'universal' rather than Greek in his habits; for example, he adopted Persian dress and customs. After his death – perhaps poisoned – his generals fought over his empire.

ROMAN REPUBLIC & JUDEA

250–198 Judea part of Ptolemaic empire based in Egypt.
241 Peace between Rome and Carthage. Carthage gives up Sicily – Sicily the first Roman province.
238 Carthage begins conquest of Spain.
218–201 Second Punic War – Hannibal (247–183) crosses Alps and defeats Romans at Ticinus and Trebia.
217 Hannibal defeats Romans at Trasimene.
216 Hannibal wins battle of Cannae.
215 Hannibal defeated by Marcellus at Nola.
215–205 First Macedonian War – Macedonia, in Greece, supports Carthage against Rome.
206 Scipio Africanus (237–183) defeats Carthaginians, under Hannibal, in Spain.
200–196 Second Macedonian War – Rome gains Greece.
198–166 Judea part of Seleucid empire under Antiochus III and IV.
183 Hannibal commits suicide while in exile in Crete, to avoid being handed over to the Romans.
167 Antiochus IV persecutes Jews.
Jewish revolt under Judas Maccabeus lasts until 164BC when Jewish worship restored.
171–167 Third Macedonian War, Macedonians led by Perseus.
149–148 Fourth Macedonian War – Macedonia again conquered.
149–146 Third Punic War – Romans destroy Carthage under Scipio the Younger (185–129).
141 Judea proclaimed an independent kingdom.
89 General Sulla regains control of rebelling Italian cities.
All Italians granted Roman citizenship.
87 Sulla defeats Mithridates and takes Athens.
82 Sulla, dictator of Rome.
78 Death of Sulla – revolt of Lepidus defeated by Pompey.
73–71 Spartacus leads slave revolt – crushed by Pompey and Crassus.
67 Civil war in Judea between Hyrcanus II and his brother Aristobulus II.
63 Jerusalem falls to Pompey. Judea annexed to Rome.
60 Triumvirate of Caesar, Pompey and Crassus rules Rome.
58 Caesar, governor of Gaul.
54 Caesar invades Britain. He leaves again but forces British chief, Cassivellaunus, to pay tribute to Rome.
52 Pompey sole consul at Rome, Caesar defeats Vercingetorix of Gaul.
50 Rivalry between Caesar and Pompey comes to a head.
49 Senate orders Caesar to relinquish the command of Gaul.
Caesar crosses River Rubicon into Italy to start civil war.
48 Caesar defeats Pompey at Pharsala in Greece. Pompey flees to Egypt, where he is murdered on Cleopatra's orders in 47.
44 Assassination of Caesar – Mark Antony (83–30) seizes power.
43 Triumvirate of Octavian, Anthony and Lepidus.
42 Caesar declared a god. His murderers, Brutus and Cassius, defeated at battle of Philippi.
37–4 Herod the Great, king of Judea.
31 Octavian defeats Antony's fleet at Actium.
30 Suicide of Antony and Cleopatra.
Egypt becomes a Roman province.
27 Octavian given supreme power in Rome and title of Augustus.
c4 Birth of Jesus Christ.
4 Death of Herod the Great – Judea split between his three sons.

CHINA

221–207 Ch'in dynasty established by Shih Huang Ti. Empire is organized into 36 provinces each under civil, military and supervisory officials. Standardization of laws and regulations.
214 Convict labour starts construction of Great Wall to keep out the Hsiung-nu (Huns).
213 Ban on books with exception of scientific works and those kept by officials. Roll silk used for writing – standardization and simplification of script.
202–AD9 Han dynasty.
191 The ban on old literature withdrawn – scholars begin to transcribe it into the new script.
155–130 Liu An directs a compilation of early philosophies, especially Taoist.
140–87 Emperor Wu Ti expands the empire. Establishment of Confucian scholarship as qualification for government administrator.
121–119 Hsiung-nu driven north of Gobi desert.
111–110 Subjugation of eastern and southern Yueh and the south west (China then covered about the same area as it does now).
Chinese traders travel Indian Ocean during following century.
108 Wu Ti conquers Choson, Korea.
100–1 Period of great literary importance – Shih Chi (Historical Memoirs) – first general history of China. Compilation of standard religious texts. First classicical inventory of extant literature.
87 Death of Wu Ti. Disorder follows.

ANCIENT CHINA

By 1100BC the Chinese had established a civilization along their great rivers for more than four centuries. Shih Huang Ti who founded the Ch'in dynasty (221–207 BC) established a framework of government which was to last for 2000 years. He brought six squabbling Chinese states under his rule in a single empire which he then divided into provinces. He created uniform standards throughout the empire – weights and measures, writing and laws. He built the Wall, China's greatest monument which still stands today, to control and keep out the barbarian Huns to the north. Over the next two centuries China established a system of officials (civil servants) trained according to the teachings of Confucius to run this huge empire.

Paper making was one of the great technical achievements of the Chinese Han dynasty (202–9BC). The Chinese also knew how to melt iron and forge it and how to cure diseases by acupuncture (still used today).

A Chinese sedan chair, AD125. It was carried by four servants.

A Chinese abacus. The abacus is still used in many parts of the world today.

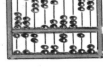

A Chinese peasant's homestead. The roofs of the living areas are made of tiles. The watchtowers are constantly manned to look out for robbers.

The Chinese invented this chain pump to irrigate their land from the Yellow River in the 2nd century BC.

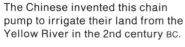

The wheelbarrow was invented in China in the 3rd century AD it was first used to carry people.

A Chinese market, AD100. The man in the tower bangs a drum when business must close for the day.

THE ROMAN WORLD

From small beginnings in Italy the Romans spread their rule throughout the Mediterranean world. The Romans were soldiers, traders, lawgivers and builders. Their laws provided a framework for Europe long after the empire had collapsed and their roads and buildings were some of the finest ever constructed. Under Trajan (98–117) Rome reached its greatest extent, stretching from Britain to the Tigris. Four emperors – Trajan, Hadrian, Antonius Pius and Marcus Aurelius (the philosopher emperor) – who ruled from 98 to 180 – presided over the Golden Age of Rome.

EARLY CHRISTIANITY

In the two centuries following the death of Jesus Christ the new religion of Christianity spread rapidly throughout the Mediterranean world. Its main appeal was to the poor, the powerless and slaves. Paul spent 30 years teaching Christ's message after his conversion in 32AD. The first gospel (St Mark's) was witten about 65AD. Peter and Paul were both martyred in Rome which became the heart of Christendom. Persecution of Christians began in 64AD by the Emperor Nero and under the Emperor Constantine in 313.

THE ROMAN EMPIRE AD 117

Eburacum
Lindum
Camulodunum
Londinium
Rhine
Colonia Agrippinensium
Augusta Trevorum
Lutetia
Aventicum
Comum
Verona
Lugdunum
Nemausus
Narbo
Massilia
Roma
Segovia
Caesaraugusta
Toletum
Neapolis
Pompeii
Tarentum
Olispo
Corduba
Malaca
Carthago Nova
Messania
Syracusae
Carthago
MEDITERRANEAN SEA
Tingis
Lambaesis
Lepcis Magna
BLACK SEA
Danube
Epidamnos
Byzantium
Ancyra
Thessalonica
Pergamum
Ephesus
Miletus
Athenae
Epidaurus
Xanthus
Tarsus
Antiochia
Seleucia
Laodicea
Palmyra
Damascus
Caesarea
Jerusalem
Alexandria
Cyrene
Appolonia
Memphis

A Roman legionary wore an iron helmet and over his woollen tunic armour of overlapping iron scales.

Above left: A Roman *testudo* (the Latin word for tortoise) a way of advancing under a hail of arrows and stones.

Gladiators fighting starving lions was a popular sport in ancient Rome. The gladiators were usually slaves or criminals.

A Roman *domus*. The main rooms of the house have under-floor heating. Notice the raised pavement for pedestrians.

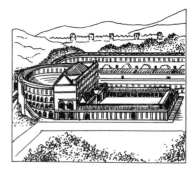

A Roman theatre at Orange in France. Actors wore large masks depicting the character they were playing.

ROME & CHRISTIANITY

5 Rome acknowledges Cymbeline king of Britain.
14 Death of Augustus. Tiberius Caesar succeeds.
18 Death of poet, Ovid.
26–36 Pontius Pilate procurator of Judea.
27 Baptism of Jesus by John the Baptist.
30 Christ crucified.
31 Martyrdom of St Stephen.
32 Saul converted to Christianity – becomes 'Paul'.
37–44 Herod Agrippa is king of northern Palestine.
37 Death of Tiberius. Gaius 'Caligula' succeeds.
41 Assassination of Caligula; Claudius emperor.
43 Romans under Aulus Plautius invade Britain.
54 Claudius murdered. Nero becomes emperor.
60 Paul on trial before the Roman procurator, Festus.
61 Boadicea of the Iceni leads a revolt in Britain. Put down with great severity by Suetonius Paulinus. Boadicea dies.
64 Fire destroys Rome – Christians blamed.
64 St Peter executed.
65 St Mark's Gospel.
67 Martyrdom of St Paul.
68 Rebellion at Rome. Nero commits suicide – Year of the Four Emperors with Galba, Otho, Vitellius.
69–79 Vespasian defeats Vitellius to become emperor.
70 Titus (Vespasian's son) captures and destroys Jerusalem and suppresses Jewish revolt. First *diaspora* (expulsion of Jews). St Matthew's Gospel.
73 Jewish stronghold at Masada falls to Romans.
75 St Luke's Gospel.
77–84 Agricola governor of Britain – completes conquest.
79–81 Emperor Titus.
79 Vesuvius destroys Pompeii, Herculaneum and Stabiae.
81 Death of Titus – Domitian succeeds.
95 St John's Gospel and Book of Revelation
96 Assassination of Domitian. Nerva emperor to 98.
98–117 Trajan – the last period of Roman expansion.
116 Tigris becomes the eastern frontier of the empire.
117–138 Emperor Hadrian.
122 Hadrian, in Britain, commences building of the wall.
132 Jewish revolt establishes an independent state in Israel. Jerusalem captured.
135 Final *diaspora* of Jews.
138 Death of Hadrian. Antoninus Pius succeeds.
161 Death of Antoninus Pius. Marcus Aurelius succeeds.
180 Death of Marcus Aurelius.
180–192 Emperor Commodus.
193–211 African-born Septimius Severus, seizes Rome.
212–217 Emperor Caracalla – extended citizenship to all free inhabitants of the empire.
218–222 Emperor Elagabulus – introduces a form of sun worship.
222–235 Emperor Alexander Severus.
235–238 Emperor Maximinius.
238–244 Emperor Gordian.
244–249 Emperor Philip the Arab.
249–251 Emperor Decius.
250 Emperor worship made compulsory.

CHINA

9–23 Wang Mang establishes the short Hsia dynasty.
25–220 Later Han dynasty.
58 Emperor Ming-ti introduces Buddhism to China.
74–94 Pan Ch'ao brings petty states of Turkestan into submission and so opens silk trade to the Roman empire.
82–132 Empire is dominated and ruled by women.
105–121 Dowager Empress Teng rules.
144–150 Empress Liang rules on behalf of three boy emperors.
150 Korea independent from China.
166 Emperor Huang-ti receives gifts from the Roman Emperor Marcus Aurelius.
189 Massacre of the Eunuchs by Yüan Shao.
189–220 Hsien-ti, weak last emperor of the Han dynasty.
220–264 Empire divided into three kingdoms. Loyang the capital. Eunuchs excluded from government.
221–264 Shu-Han dynasty.
222–264 Wu dynasty founded by Sun Ch'uan in the lower Long River Valley: capital at Chien-K'ang (Nanking).
230 Accession of Sujin, 10th Emperor of Japan. The beginning of historical records in Japan.

ROME IN DECLINE

268 Major Goth invasion – Athens, Corinth and Sparta sacked.
284–305 Emperor Diocletian.
286 Diocletian divides the empire for ease of government. Diocletian rules the eastern half, Maximian the west.
287 Carausius, commander of the Roman British fleet, revolts in Britain and rules independently to 293. He is murdered by co-rebel Allectus.
305 Diocletian and Maximian abdicate.
Power struggle follows.
306–337 Constantine the Great, emperor in the east.
308–312 Maxentius, emperor in the west.
312 Battle of Milvian Bridge – Constantine defeats Maxentius.
Constantine is converted to Christianity.
313 Edict of Toleration proclaimed at Milan – Christianity allowed by Constantine.
324 Constantine reunites the empire.
330 Constantine founds Constantinople, at Byzantium, to be capital of the empire.
337 Constantine baptized on his deathbed.
361–363 Emperor Julian reverts to paganism.
364–375 Valentine, emperor in the west.
364–378 Valens, emperor in the east.
375–383 Emperor Gratian (west).
378 Defeat and death of Valens at Adrianople (W. Turkey) at hands of Goths.
379–395 Theodosius the Great (east).
Constantinople is now the real centre of imperial power.
383–388 Magnus Maximus (west). His legions begin to leave Britain to conquer Gaul and Spain, but he is executed by Theodosius.
394 Theodosius briefly reunites the empire.
He forbids the Olympic Games.
395–397 Stilicho, Vandal leader of Roman forces, drives Visigoths from Roman Greece.
401–417 Pope Innocent I claims universal jurisdiction over Roman Church.
406 Vandals overrun Gaul.
407 Last Roman troops leave Britain.
408–450 Theodosius II, emperor of the east.
410 Alaric of the Goths sacks Rome.
425 Founding of Constantinople University.
425–455 Emperor Valentinian III (west).
433–453 Attila leads the Huns.
439 Gaiseric of the Vandals captures Carthage.
440–461 Pope Leo the Great.
450–457 Emperor Marcian (east).
452 Attila invades northern Italy.
Venice is founded by refugees from the Huns.
455 Gaiseric of the Vandals attacks Rome.
457–475 Emperor Leo I (east).
475–476 Romulus Augustulus last emperor in the west.
476 He is deposed by the Goths under Odovacar – end of the western empire.
Eastern empire continues under Teno and Anastarius and lasts for 1000 more years.
481 Clovis, king of the Franks.
493 Theodoric of the Ostrogoths becomes king of all Italy.

PERSIA & INDIA

240–271 Shapur I founds the powerful neo-Persian empire of the Sassanids.
296–297 Persia at war with Rome. At the peace Rome gives Mesopotamia to Persia. River Tigris becomes boundary between two empires.
309–379 Shapur II of Persia.
320–330 Chandragupta I founds Gupta dynasty in India which lasts to 525.
330–375 Samudragupta, emperor of India – patron of poetry and music; extends empire to the north west.
337–350 Shapur II at war with eastern Roman strongholds – fails to capture them.
339 Persecution of Persian Christians.
359–361 Shapur II again goes to war against Rome. But repulsed by Emperor Julian in 363.
371–376 Third war with Rome under Shapur II – indecisive, but Persian power reaches its zenith.
379 Death of Shapur II followed by a series of weak rulers.
409–416 Persian Christians allowed to worship openly.
420–440 Varaharan V of Persia declares war on Rome when Persian Christians cross border seeking Theodosius' protection.
440–457 Yezdigird II of Persia, forcibly converts Armenia to Zoroastrianism.
477–496 Buddhagupta – last emperor of the Indian Gupta dynasty.
483–485 Volagases of Persia grants Edict of Toleration to Christians of Armenia and its regions.

THE MIDDLE AGES AD500–1100

The collapse of the Roman Empire led to a period of great confusion throughout Europe – sometimes described as the Dark Ages – before the new medieval order was to emerge. Christianity gradually became the basis of western life. In the Middle East the new religion of Islam was carried far and wide by Arab warriors.

A Viking ship sets sail for new lands carrying everything they may need. The colonists ships were strong and seaworthy, but very uncomfortable.

EUROPE

503 Battle of Mount Badon – Arthur the Briton defeats Saxons from Germany.

584 Anglo-Saxon kingdom of Mercia is founded in England.

664 Synod of Whitby – Oswy of Northumbria accepts Rome's form of Christianity.

710–711 Roderic, the last Visigoth king of Spain. Moors invade Spain.

732 Charles Martel, ruler of the Franks, holds Moors at Tours because Martel's cavalry is equipped with stirrups allowing more effective use of sword and spear.

751 Pépin the Short, ruler of the Franks founds the Carolingian dynasty.

771–814 Charlemagne, king of the Franks.

787 First Danish invasion of Britain.

796 Death of Offa ends Mercian supremacy in England.

800 Pope Leo III crowns Charlemagne first Holy Roman emperor.

800–850 Feudalism – the granting of land by a powerful person to a less powerful man in return for service – established by the Franks mainly for military purposes.

Horses bred as big as possible for war.

843 Treaty of Verdun – division of Frankish (Holy Roman) empire. Louis the German rules east of the Rhine, Charles the Bald rules France, Lothair rules Italy, Provence, Burgundy, Lorraine.

851 Crossbow used in France.

871–899 Alfred the Great, king of Wessex.

900 Alfonso III of Castille begins to reconquer Spain from the Moors.

Castles become seats of the European nobility.

911 Hrolf the Ganger is granted Normandy.

936–973 Otto I, the Great, king of Germany revives Holy Roman empire and in 962 has himself crowned Emperor Augustus, founding a line of emperors which endure until Napoleon I abolishes the empire in 1806.

982 Eric the Red settles Greenland.

1016 Danes rule England.

1066 Norman conquest of England.

1075 Dispute between pope and emperor over which ruler should appoint bishops.

1096–1122 First Crusade follows an appeal by Pope Urban to free the Holy Places.

ELSEWHERE

527–565 Justinian, emperor of Byzantium (eastern Roman empire).

570 Birth of Muhammad at Mecca.

585 Reconstruction of Great Wall of China.

618 T'ai Tsu founds the Tang dynasty in China.

625 Muhammad begins dictating the Koran.

632 Death of Muhammad.

635 Muslims begin conquest of Syria and Persia.

642 Fall of Persia and Egypt to Muslims.

661–750 Omayyad dynasty in Islam founded by Caliph Muawiya.

668 Korea united under Silla.

674 Arab conquest reaches River Indus in India.

675 First Bulgar empire south of the River Danube.

700 Arabs capture Tunis – virtual end of Christianity in north Africa.

751 Arabs defeat Chinese at Samarkand.

786–809 Harun al-Raschid, caliph of Baghdad.

850 Citadel built in Zimbabwe.

880 Basil, emperor of Byzantium, drives Arabs from mainland Italy.

922 Fatimids seize Morocco.

960 Sung dynasty in China (to 1275).

976–997 T'ai Tsung completes re-union of China.

980 Arabs settle the east coast of Africa.

999 Bagauda, first king of Kano in northern Nigeria.

1061 Establishment of the Almoravid dynasty in north Africa – the conquest of Spain follows.

1071 Battle of Manzikert – Seljuk Turk leader, Alp Arslan, defeats Byzantine army and conquers Asia Minor.

1090 Foundation of the Assassin sect in Persia.

1099 Crusaders capture Jerusalem.

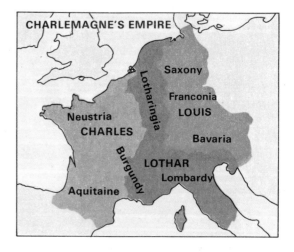

How Charlemagne's empire was divided among his grandsons. Charles's inheritance became modern France and that of Louis was the basis of modern Germany.

TRAVEL & TRADE

500 Stirrup starting to be used – at first for greater comfort when riding, later used in battle.
800 onwards. Lateen (triangular) sail used in the Mediterranean. Made it possible for boats to beat into the wind.
800–900 Growth of trans-Sahara trade in Africa.
890 Nailed horseshoes first used allowing long journeys – cheap enough to be afforded by peasants for agricultural use.
900 Mayas emigrate into Yucatan.
Vikings develop the art of shipbuilding and discover Greenland.
907 Commercial treaties between Kiev and Constantinople.

The prophet Muhammad before the battle of Uheed in 625. Following Muslim tradition Muhammad's face is veiled.

950 Padded horsecollar means horses can pull heavier loads and wagons. Previously harnessed with a breast-band which choked the horse when pulling heavy loads.
Kupe, the great Polynesian navigator, discovers New Zealand on canoe voyage.
982 Viking, Eric the Red settles Greenland.
983 Venice and Genoa trade with Asia.
1000 Viking, Biarni Heriulfsson is blown off course and sights North America.
1002 Leif Ericsson (son of Eric the Red) journeys down the American coast possibly as far as Maryland.

CULTURE & RELIGION

529 Monastery of Monte Cassino, Italy, founded by St Benedict of Nursia. Although they lead a life of prayer and manual labour, the monks provide almost all medical skill and preserve much classical learning that would otherwise be lost.
529–565 Codification of Byzantine laws under Justinian. Byzantine empire has own form of Christianity, preserved as the Eastern Orthodox Church.
550 St David brings Christianity to Wales.
552 Buddhism reaches Japan.
563 St Columba converts the Picts from Scotland to Christianity and founds monastery on the island of Iona off the west coast of Scotland.
597 St Augustine converts the kingdom of Kent to Christianity.
610 Vision of Muhammad when Angel Gabriel commands him to proclaim the one true God, Allah.
622 The *Hegira* – Muhammad flees to Medina from persecution in Mecca.
624 Buddhism becomes the official religion of China.
700 Translation of the psalms into Anglo-Saxon – the Lindisfarne Gospels.
731 Bede's *Ecclesiastical history of the church in England.*
782 onwards. Revival of learning in Europe under Charlemagne.
841–846 Wu Tsung persecutes all religions in China except Buddhism.
891 Alfred begins the *Anglo-Saxon Chronicle* – a history of England.
910 Foundation of Cluny Abbey in France – epitomizes the Romanesque style of architecture.
932 Wood block printing is adopted in China allowing mass production of books.
978 Chinese begin the compilation of 1000 volume history.
988 Vladimir of Kiev introduces Eastern Orthodox religion to his lands.
993 Olaf Skutkonnung – the first Christian king of Sweden.
995–1028 Golden Age of the arts in Japan.
1000 Widespread fear of the 'End of the World' and the 'Last Judgement'.
1052 Edward the Confessor founds new Westminster Abbey.
1054 Final break between Roman and Byzantine churches.
1076 Synod of Worms – bishops depose Pope Gregory; beginning of a power struggle between popes and Holy Roman emperors.
1086 *Domesday Book.*

WEST EUROPE

511 Death of Clovis, the Frankish king – his empire divided between his four sons – the Meroving dynasty starts.
561 Civil war breaks out between the Merovings.
568 Lombards under Alcuin conquer northern Italy.
584 Anglo-Saxon kingdom of Mercia.
629 Dagobert I re-unites the Frankish kingdom.
655 Oswy, king of Northumbria defeats and kills Penda of Mercia.
687 Pépin the Younger re-unites the Frankish kingdom after the battle of Tertry.
710–711 Roderic – last Visigoth king of Spain. Moors invade Spain – Roderic defeated; end of Visigoth monarchy.
718 Pelayo, a Visigoth, founds the kingdom of Asturias in the Spanish mountains. Moors hold the rest of peninsula.
732 Charles Martel, ruler of the Franks, holds the Muslim Moors at the battle of Tours.
751 Pépin the Short crowned king of the Franks – founds Carolingian dynasty to replace Merovingian dynasty.
757 Offa, king of Mercia builds his dyke to keep out the Welsh.
771–814 Charlemagne (Pepin's son), king of the Franks.
772 Charlemagne conquers Saxony in Germany and converts it to Christianity.
778 Battle of Roncesvalles – Moors and Basques ambush the Franks.
779 Offa of Mercia becomes king of all England.
782 Revival of learning in Europe under Charlemagne who summons Alcuin of York (monk and scholar) to head palace school at Aachen.
787 First Danish invasion of Britain.
800 Pope Leo III, in gratitude for protecting and expanding Christian Europe, crowns Charlemagne Holy Roman emperor of the west.

ISLAM

570 Birth of Muhammad at Mecca.
610 Vision of Muhammad.
622 The *Hegira* – Muhammad flees from persecution in Mecca to Yathrib (Medina).
625 Muhammad begins dictating the *Koran.*
630 Muhammad captures Mecca – principles of Islam set out.
632 Death of Muhammad.
634–644 Omar I, caliph of Mecca. Holy War against Persians.
635–641 Muslims commence conquest of Syria.
638 Muslims capture Jerusalem.
639–642 Muslims conquer Egypt.
645 Byzantines recapture Alexandria – people rise against Arabs.
646 Arabs recapture Alexandria.
655 First Arab naval victory – battle of the Masts at which Byzantines are defeated off Alexandria.
661 Muawiya, caliph to 680, founds the Omayyad dynasty – to 750.
673–678 Arabs besiege Constantinople but without success.
680 Arab civil war.
697 Arabs destroy Carthage.
700 Arabs capture Tunis – virtual end of Christianity in north Africa.
702 Arabic made official language of Egypt.
707 Arabs capture Tangier.
712 Muslim state established in Sind.
716–717 Arabs besiege Constantinople – fail to take it.
751 Arabs defeat Chinese at Samarkand.
756 Omayyad dynasty established at Cordoba in Spain by Ad-al-Rahman ibn Mu'awiya.
767–772 Christian Coptic revolt in Egypt.
786–809 Haroun-al-Raschid, caliph of Baghdad.

ISLAM

Muhammad, the founder of the religion Islam was born at Mecca in 570. Forced to flee to Medina in 622 because of his beliefs, he dictated the Koran (the Holy Book of the Muslim faith) before leading his followers back to capture Mecca in 630. Over the next two hundred years the desert Arabs of Arabia were to carry Islam by the sword across north Africa and into Spain, north into Syria and Turkey and east as far as Sind (Pakistan). Their great cities – Damascus, Baghdad, Cordoba – became centres of magnificence and learning.

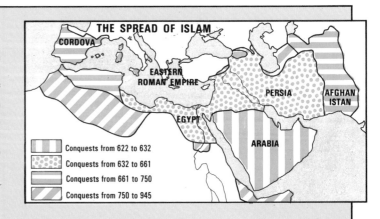

THE SPREAD OF ISLAM

Conquests from 622 to 632
Conquests from 632 to 661
Conquests from 661 to 750
Conquests from 750 to 945

BYZANTIUM

500–642 Constant fighting between Byzantium and Persia.
527–565 Justinian, emperor of Byzantium.
529–565 Justinian has Byzantine laws codified.
534 Belisarius, the Byzantine general conquers Vandals of north Africa.
535–554 Byzantium reconquers Italy.
542–546 Plague spreads in Byzantine empire.
565–578 Justin II, emperor of Byzantium.
572–628 Persians control Arabia.
589 Arabs, Khazars and Turks invade Persia and are defeated.
626 Emperor Heraclius of Byzantium expels Persians from Egypt.
642 Final defeat of Persians by Arabs at Nehawand.
710 Justinian II confirms papal privileges.
726 Pope Gregory II opposes iconoclasm (violent Byzantine movement against sacred images started by Emperor Leo III).
733 Emperor Leo III withdraws Byzantine provinces from papal jurisdiction.
787 Council of Nicaea – restoration of images in churches.
797 Empress Irene has her son Constantine blinded and rules to 802 when deposed.

AFRICA & THE EAST

496–534 N. Africa: Vandals rule.
534–550 China: Eastern Wei dynasty.
550–577 China: The Northern Ch'i dynasty.
562 Korea: End of Japanese power.
589 China re-united by Wen Ti who founds Sui dynasty.
593–628 Suiko, empress of Japan. Buddhism takes root and Japan is much influenced by Chinese civilization.
604 Japan gets her first written constitution.
605–610 China: Building of Grand Canal.
618–907 China: T'ang dynasty founded by T'ai Tsung.
627–649 T'ai Tsung, the Great, emperor of China – a period of military conquest, patronage of arts and letters.
700–800 Bantu Africans cross the River Limpopo taking Iron Age to the south.

THE MONASTERIES

In the Europe of the Middle Ages monasteries were centres of great wealth; the power of their abbots rivalled that of the great barons. Few people outside the church could read or write so that monasteries with their libraries became the main centres of learning. Monasteries provided help for the poor and sick and hospitality for wanderers, acting as early guesthouses. There were different orders of monks and the various monasteries reflected this: some were famous for teaching, others for the simplicity of their way of life. Of the several orders of monks the Benedictines were the most widespread. In 529 Benedict of Nursia founded the abbey of Monte Cassino, south of Rome. Benedict wrote a famous Rule which influenced religious communities of men and women for centuries.

Monks in the *scriptorium* or writing room. Monasteries were centres of learning as well as being the hotels and hospitals of the time.

EUROPE

814–840 Political importance of western empire on decline after Charlemagne's death.
Louis the Pious, son of Charlemagne, emperor and king of the Franks.
828 Egbert of Wessex becomes the overall ruler of England.
838 Louis the Pious divides the Frankish empire between his three sons – Lothair, Louis the German, Charles the Bald.
843 Treaty of Verdun – Frankish empire is re-divided. Three Carolingian dynasties – Louis the German rules east of the Rhine, Charles the Bald rules France, Lothair rules Italy, Provence, Burgundy and Lorraine.
844 Kenneth MacAlpine, king of the Scots, defeats the Picts and founds a united Scotland.
861 Vikings discover Iceland.
865 Vikings invade England – conquer Northumbria, East Anglia, Mercia.
865–871 Ethelred I, king of Wessex.
871 Danes attack Wessex.
871–899 Alfred the Great, last son of Ethelwulf, king of Wessex.
874 Vikings settle in Iceland.
878 Battle of Edington – Alfred inflicts a decisive defeat on the Danes.
Treaty of Wedmore divides England – Wessex in the south and the Danes in the north – beginning of Danelaw.
881 Charles III, the Fat, emperor and king of Germany, becomes also king of the Franks and re-unites the empire of Charlemagne.
889 Magyars under Arpad invade Hungarian plain.
899 Alfred's death – Edward the Elder becomes king of Wessex.
900 Alfonso III, the Great, of Castille begins to reconquer Spain from the Moors.
906 Magyars begin to invade Germany.
911 Viking Rollo (Hrolf the Ganger) is granted Normandy by the Franks.
912 Rollo is baptized and takes the name Robert.
924–939 Athelstan, king of Wessex, comes to rule most of England.
929 Murder of Wenceslas of Bohemia by his younger brother after attempting to convert his people to Christianity.
936–973 Otho I (the Great), king of Germany.
937 Battle of Brunanburh – Athelstan defeats an alliance of Scots, Celts, Danes, Vikings.
939–946 Edmund, brother of Athelstan, king of England.
942–953 Malcolm I, king of Scots.
946–955 Edred, younger brother of Edmund, king of England.
950 Otto I conquers Bohemia.

ELSEWHERE

740–1036 North India: Gurjaru-Prathi-Nara dynasty.
800 Africa: Ghana already known as the 'Land of Gold'.
800–900 Africa: Growth of trans-Sahara trade between west and north Africa – development of cities such as Gao.
800–950 North India: Many petty states exist.
803 Islam: Harun al-Raschid ends the power of the Barmecide family in Baghdad.
813–833 Islam: Mamun the Great, caliph of Baghdad – liberal religious attitudes, a great artistic period.
841–846 China: Wu Tsung initiates persecutions of all religions except Buddhism which is allowed to survive.
862 Russia: Rurik, with the Viking tribe of Russ, seizes power in northern Russia and founds Novgorod.
865 Russia: Russian Vikings attack Constantinople.
867 Byzantium: Photian Schism – the Byzantine Church under Photius, the patriarch of Constantinople, challenges the authority of the pope. In 879 they excommunicate each other.
869 Islam: Arabs conquer Malta.
880 Byzantium: Emperor Basil drives Arabs from mainland Italy.
900 Africa: Hausa kingdom of Daura founded in northern Nigeria.
Zimbabwe in southern Africa a major power.
Byzantium: Bulgars accept the Eastern Orthodox religion.
Islam: The beginnings of the famous Arabian tales: *'A Thousand and One Nights'*.
907 China: End of T'ang dynasty is followed by civil wars which last to 960.
907–1123 China: Mongol expansion in Inner Mongolia and northern China.
908–932 Islam: Caliph Muqtadir – the Fatimids conquer north Africa.
916 Africa: Al-Masudi, the Arab scholar, travels from the Gulf down the African coast as far as Mozambique.
920 Africa: Golden Age of Ghana begins.
922 Africa: Fatimids seize Morocco.
930 Islam: Cordoba in Spain becomes the seat of Arab learning.
932 China: Wood block printing adopted to mass-produce classical books – a cheap substitute for stone engraving. Nine Classics are printed.
939 Japan: Civil war.

955–959 Edwy, son of Edmund, king of England.

957 Mercia and Northumbria rebel against Edwy.

959–975 Edgar, brother of Edwy, king of England.

971–995 Kenneth II, king of Scots.

975–978 Edward the Martyr, king of England.

978–1016 Ethelred II succeeds Edward the Martyr.

980 Danes raid England.

991 Battle of Maldon – Byrhtnoth of Essex defeated by Danes.

992 Ethelred concludes a truce with Duke Richard I of Normandy.

994 Sweyn of Denmark and Olaf Trygvesson of Norway sail up the Thames to besiege London.

1002 Ethelred marries Emma, sister of Duke Richard of Normandy.
Massacre of St Brice's day – Ethelred orders the slaughter of all Danes in southern England.

1003 Sweyn lands in England to avenge the massacre.

1013 Sweyn lands in England and is proclaimed king – Ethelred flees to Normandy.

1014 Ethelred II is recalled on the death of Sweyn. Canute retreats to Denmark.

1015 Canute the Dane invades England.

1016 Edmund Ironside, king of England, divides it with Canute who holds the north while Edmund holds Wessex. Edmund is assassinated.

1016–1035 Canute, king of England.

1017 Canute divides England into four earldoms.

1019 Canute marries Emma, widow of Ethelred II.

1034–1040 Duncan, king of Scots.

1035–1040 Harold I Harefoot, king of England.

1040–1042 Hardicanute, king of England and Denmark.

1040–1057 Macbeth, king of Scots.

1042–1066 Edward the Confessor, king of England – power in the hands of Earl Godwin of Wessex.

1051 Godwin exiled – returns with fleet to win back power.

1052 Edward the Confessor founds new Westminster Abbey.

1053 Godwin's son Harold succeeds as earl of Wessex.

1055 Harold's brother, Tostig, becomes earl of Northumbria.

1057 Malcolm, son of Duncan, defeats and kills Macbeth. Lulac, Macbeth's son, is king for a year.

1058–1093 Malcolm Canmore, king of Scots.

1061 Malcolm invades Northumbria.

1063 Harold and Tostig subdue Wales.

1064 Harold is shipwrecked in Normandy and reluctantly swears to support William of Normandy's claim to England.

1065 Northumbria rebels and Tostig is exiled.

1066 Harold, king of England. Tostig and Harold Hardrada king of Norway (1046–66) invade England – they are defeated and killed by Harold at Stamford Bridge.
Battle of Hastings – William defeats and kills Harold to become William I, king of England to 1087.

1066–1069 William completes conquest of England.

1070 Saxons revolt under Hereward the Wake in the Fens.

1072 William invades Scotland.

1087–1100 William II (Rufus), king of England; elder brother Robert is Duke of Normandy.

1093–1097 Donald Bane king of Scots.

1097–1107 Edgar, king of Scotland.

The Norman conquest of England was a turning point for Europe. William, Duke of Normandy, had a doubtful claim to the English throne but he made it good when he defeated Harold at the Battle of Hastings in 1066. The Normans only completed the conquest of England in 1071 when Hereward the Wake submitted. They provided strong rule and unity so that for a time under William's successors England became the most powerful state in Europe. The Domesday Book (1086) is one of the earliest examples of a national census.

EUROPE

955 Battle of Lechfeld – Otto I defeats Magyars and stops their westward advance.
960–992 Mieszko I, first ruler of Poland.
962 Pope John XII crowns Otto, emperor in Rome.
987–996 Hugh Capet elected king of France – founds Capetian dynasty.
998–1038 Stephen I (St Stephen), first king of Hungary.
999 Poles conquer Silesia.
1000 Battle of Svolder – Sweyn kills Olaf of Norway and annexes Norway to Denmark.
1027–1035 Robert (the Devil), duke of Normandy.
1028 Denmark under Canute conquers Norway and his son Sweyn becomes king.
1031–1060 Henry I, king of France.
1035 William becomes duke of Normandy.
1058–1079 Boleslav II, the Bold, king of Poland, conquers Upper Slovakia.
1060–1108 Philip I, king of France.
1072–1091 Normans invade and conquer Sicily.
1076 Synod of Worms – bishops declare Pope Gregory deposed – Gregory excommunicates Henry IV.
1077 The Holy Roman Emperor, Henry IV, his throne threatened, does penance to pope at Canossa.
1077–1080 Civil war in the Holy Roman empire.
1080 Pope Gregory again excommunicates Henry and declares him deposed.
1083 Henry IV storms Rome.
1084 Robert Guiscard, duke of Apulia, forces Henry to retreat to Germany.
1085 Spain: Alfonso VI captures Toledo from the Moors.
1086 Canute IV of Denmark assassinated – threat to England is lifted.

AFRICA & ASIA

960–1275 China: Sung dynasty.
972 China: Buddhist Canon is printed in Szechuan.
976–997 China: T'ai Tsung completes reunion.
995–1028 Japan: Rule of the Fujiwara Michinaga clan – a literary and artistic golden age.
998–1030 Mahmud, Turkish ruler of Ghazni, founds empire in northern India and eastern Afghanistan.
999 Africa: Bagauda, first king of Kano, in northern Nigeria.
1000 Chinese perfect their invention of gunpowder. Ghana at the height of its power – controls Atlantic ports and trade routes across the Sahara.
1018 India: Mahmud of Ghazni pillages the sacred city of Muttra.
1021 Islam: Caliph al-Hakim declares himself divine – founds the Druse sect.
1028–1050 Zoe, empress of Byzantine empire.

1054 Africa: Abdullah ben Yassim begins the Muslim conquest of west Africa.
1061 Establishment of the Muslim Almoravid dynasty in north Africa – conquest of Spain follows.
1063 Africa: Ghana under Tunka Manin – can field an army of 200,000.
1069–1072 Famine in Egypt.
1071 Turkey: Battle of Manzikert – Alp Arslan, the Seljuk Turk, defeats the Byzantine army and conquers most of Asia Minor.
1075 Seljuk Malik Shah conquers Syria and Palestine.
1090 Hasan ibn al-Sabbah, first Old Man of the Mountain, founds Assassin sect in Persia.
1098 Crusaders defeat the Muslim Saracens at Antioch.
1099 Crusaders capture Jerusalem and Godfrey of Bouillon is elected king of Jerusalem.

MEDIEVAL AFRICAN EMPIRES

For centuries great empires flourished in West Africa but they were almost unknown outside the continent, isolated behind the Sahara desert. One of the greatest of these was the Empire of Ghana. It was ruled for a time by the Maga, a Berber family, though the people were Negroes of the Soninke tribes. It reached its height in the tenth and eleventh centuries when it stretched from the Atlantic to Timbuktu.

SELJUK TURKS

In the 900s Seljuk led a tribe of Turks from central Asia. They spread rapidly creating the first Turkish Empire which lasted until the early 1400s. An event of great importance was their conversion to Islam in 960. In 1071 the Seljuks won control of Asia minor. The area they occupied became known as Turkey. Conflict arose between the Seljuks and Christian pilgrims to the Holy Land. This led to the bitter conflict of the Crusades.

THE FEUDAL AGE 1100–1453

In the 12th century Constantinople again became 'the centre of the world'. In China on the other side of the world progress in the arts and sciences developed almost unknown to western civilization. In England, France, Germany, Italy and Spain the feudal system provided the structure of society until the Black Death delivered a crippling blow.

A market scene in a French town in the Middle Ages.

EUROPE & MIDDLE EAST

1104 Crusaders capture Acre.
1154–1189 Henry II of England controls half France.
1170 Murder of Thomas à Becket, (canonized in 1173).
1171 Henry II annexes Ireland.
1174 Saladin, sultan of Egypt, conquers Syria.
1187 Saladin captures Jerusalem.
1189–1192 Third Crusade.
1204 Crusaders sack Constantinople and install Latin Christian ruler.
1212 Children's Crusade – 30,000 children from France and Germany set out for Palestine. Thousands are sold into slavery.
1215 Magna Carta.
1217 Fifth Crusade ends – fails to capture Egypt.
1218 Mongols conquer Persia.
1228–1229 Sixth Crusade – recaptures Jerusalem.
1240 Mongols capture Moscow.
1241 Mongols invade Hungary and then are forced to withdraw from Europe following the death of Ogadai Khan.
1242 Batu sets up Mongol kingdom of 'Golden Horde' on lower Volga River.
1243 Egyptians capture Jerusalem from Christians.
1265 Simon de Montfort's parliament in England – leading citizens from the main towns appointed to take part.
1290–1320 Osman I founds Ottoman dynasty in Turkey.
1291 Saracens capture Acre – last Christian stronghold. End of Crusades.
1295 Edward I holds Model Parliament – Simon de Montfort's principles put into practice.

ELSEWHERE

1100 Polynesian islands colonized.
1151 Mexico: End of Toltec empire.
1156 Japan: Civil wars.
1167 Almaric, king of Jerusalem, captures Cairo.
1168 Arabs recapture Cairo.
1190 Temujin (later Genghis Khan) begins to create Mongol empire.
1210 Mongols invade China.
1227 Death of Genghis Khan.
1240 Africa: End of old Ghana empire – rise of Mali.
1260 Kublai has himself elected Khan by his army.
1247 Mongols invade Japan.
1275 Marco Polo enters service of Kublai Khan.
1294 Death of Kublai Khan.

The seal of King John on Magna Carta (Great Charter). The document guaranteed tax collection only by legal means, justice to all and no imprisonment without trial.

Muslims and Christians in battle in one of the Crusades. In 1291 the Christians were finally driven out of the Holy Land.

CULTURE & RELIGION

1100 Chanson de Roland, French heroic poem.
1119 Bologna University founded.
Foundation of Knights Templar. Specially formed to fight in the Crusades. Name came from the fact that the knights' headquarters were on the site of Solomon's Temple.
1122 Concordat of Worms.
1123 Death of Omar Khayyam – Persian poet.
1150 Founding of Paris University.
1170 Beginnings of Oxford University.
1174 'Leaning Tower' of Pisa built.
1176 Roman de Renard (Reynard the Fox) written in French.
1191 Second era of Mayan civilization.
1201 Façade of Notre-Dame in Paris.
1208–1213 Crusade against Albigensian heretics in France.
1209 Beginnings of Cambridge University.
1210 Francis of Assisi founds the Franciscan Order of friars. Friars did not withdraw from the world like the first religious orders but went out to teach and preach.
1212–1311 Rheims Cathedral built.
1215 St Dominic founds the Dominican Order of friars.
1225–1274 Thomas Aquinas, Italian theologian.
1240–1302 Cimabue, Florentine painter.
1245–1270 Choir and cloisters of Westminster Abbey built.
1248 Work begins on Moorish stronghold – the Alhambra in Granada, Spain.
1265–1321 Dante Alighieri, Italian poet.
1266–1337 Giotto, Italian painter.
1277 Roger Bacon, English Franciscan philosopher, exiled for heresy (to 1292).
1296 Building of Florence Cathedral under Arnolfo di Cambio.

DISCOVERIES

1120 Chinese invent playing cards.
1125 Earliest account of a mariner's compass by English scholar, Alexander Neckam.
1161 Explosives used in battle by Chinese. In use in Europe by 1341.
1180 Glass windows appear in English private houses.
First windmills with vertical sails in Europe.
1190 Crusaders encounter Saracen warship with centre-line rudder.
1202 Arabic numerals introduced into Europe.
1214–1294 Roger Bacon (English), greatest scientist of his time.
1233 Coal mined in Newcastle, England.
1238–1311 Arnold of Villanova, Spanish physician and alchemist, discovers poisonous property of carbon monoxide gas.
1250 Pivotal compass in common use in Mediterranean. Goose quills used for writing.
1252 Golden florins minted at Florence.
1254–1324 Marco Polo, Venetian traveller.
1260–1320 Henri de Mondeville, French surgeon and anatomist.
1289 Block printing used at Ravenna.
1290 Invention of spectacles in Italy. First mechanical clock devised by an unknown inventor.
1320 Lace first made in France and Flanders.
1328 Invention of the sawmill.

Temujin brought all Mongol tribes under his control. In 1206 he took the title Genghis Khan, which means 'the very mighty lord'. He died in 1227 and his empire was divided among his sons.

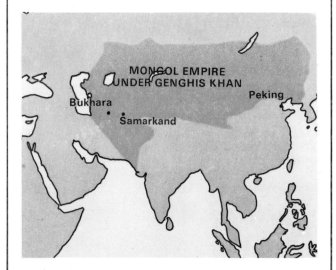

THE FEUDAL AGE 1300–1453

EUROPE

1301 Osman defeats Byzantines.
1302 Battle of Courtrai – Flemish burghers defeat French knights.
1305–1377 Popes established at Avignon.
1337 Edward III of England claims throne of France – '100 Years War' begins because of French attacks on Edward's French territories.
1344 Emergence of Hanseatic League.
1345 Ottomans cross into Europe.
1346 English defeat French at Crécy.
1348 Black Death ravages Europe.
1358 Jacquerie revolt of French peasants.
1365 Turks make Adrianople their capital.
1369 Tamerlane becomes king of Samarkand.
1381 Peasants revolt for their rights in England.
1390 Turks complete conquest of Asia Minor.
1401 Tamerlane takes Baghdad and Damascus.
1402 Tamerlane defeats Turks at Angora and overruns most of Ottoman empire.
1405 Death of Tamerlane.
1410 Battle of Tannenberg – Poles defeat Teutonic Knights.
1415 Henry V of England invades France and defeats French at Agincourt.
1420 Treaty of Troyes – Henry V is acknowledged as heir to French throne.
1431 Jeanne d'Arc (Joan of Arc) burnt as a witch at Rouen.
1451–1481 Muhammad II, sultan of Turks.
1453 Fall of Constantinople to Turks. End of Byzantine empire and the Middle Ages.
End of '100 Years War' – England retains only Calais.

ELSEWHERE

1325 Mexico: Foundation of Tenochtitlan by Aztecs.
1363 Tamerlane begins conquest of Asia.
1368 China: Foundation of Ming dynasty by Chu Yuan-chang.
1398–1399 India: Tamerlane invades kingdom of Delhi.
1421 Chinese transfer capital to Peking.
1438 S. America: Incas establish empire in Peru.

Tamerlane, the Tatar ruler and descendant of Genghis Khan.

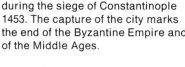

Turkish troops storming the walls during the siege of Constantinople 1453. The capture of the city marks the end of the Byzantine Empire and of the Middle Ages.

CULTURE

A woodcut of the knight from Chaucer's *Canterbury Tales*.

1304–1374 Birth of Petrarch.

1305–1377 Popes at Avignon – the 'Babylonian Captivity'. Clement V removed the papal court from Rome to southern France, to escape the political turmoil which was raging in Italy. Gregory XI transferred the papal court back to Rome.

1307–1321 Dante composes *Divine Comedy*.

1314 Completion of old St Paul's Cathedral, London.

1325 Development of Nō plays in Japan.

1340–1400 Geoffrey Chaucer, English poet.

1348–1353 Boccaccio (1313–1375) Italian poet writes the *Decameron*.

1369–1453 John Dunstable, English composer.

1375 Robin Hood appears in English popular literature.

1376 John Wyclif calls for Church reforms in England.

1378–1417 Great Schism – rival popes at Rome and Avignon.

1386–1466 Donatello, Italian sculptor.

1387–1400 Chaucer writes *The Canterbury Tales*.

1399–1474 Guillaume Dufay, Dutch composer.

1400 Modern English develops from Middle English.

1403 Compilation of *Yung Lo Ta Tien*, Chinese encyclopaedia in 22,937 volumes (only three copies made).

1414 Medici family of Florence become bankers to the papacy.

1420 Brunelleschi designs dome on Florence Cathedral.
Erection of the Great Temple of the Dragon, Peking.

1426 Holland becomes the centre of European music.

1450 Florence under the Medicis becomes centre of Renaissance and humanism.

1452–1519 Italian painter Leonardo da Vinci.

1453 Fall of Constantinople – scholars flee to the west.

DISCOVERY

1337 First scientific weather forecasts by William Merlee of Oxford.

1352 Arab geographer Ibn Battuta explores Sahara desert and visits Mali.

1360 First francs coined in France.

1370 Steel crossbow used as a weapon of war.

1396–1468 Johannes Gutenberg, German inventor of printing from movable type (1440) in Europe.

1405–1433 Cheng Ho, the Chinese explorer makes seven voyages to south-east Asia, India, Persia and Africa.

1415 Oil colours introduced in painting by Flemish artists, Jan and Hubert van Eyck.

1416 Dutch fishermen the first to use drift nets.

1430 'Mad Marjorie', the great cast iron gun, introduced.

1432–1434 Portuguese explorers discover the Azores and round Cape Bojada.

1450 Brandy claimed to have been distilled in the Duchy of Modena, Italy, for the first time.

1451–1506 Christopher Columbus, the 'discoverer of America'.

1452 Metal plates are used for printing.

A painting of Dante, Italy's greatest poet. His most famous work is *The Divine Comedy*.

THE FEUDAL AGE 1100–1200

EUROPE

1100–1135 Henry I, king of England. Youngest son of William the Conqueror crowned on assassination of William II.
1106 Battle of Tenchebrai – Henry I defeats his brother Robert, duke of Normandy and imprisons him for the rest of his life.
1106–1125 Henry V, Holy Roman emperor.
1108–1137 Louis VI, king of France.
1114 Matilda (daughter of Henry I) marries Henry V.
1115 St Bernard founds the abbey of Clairvaux in France.
1119 Hugues de Payens founds the Order of Knights Templar in Jerusalem.
1122 Concordat of Worms – German princes end the dispute between pope and emperor over appointment of bishops.
1125–1137 Lothair of Saxony elected Holy Roman emperor.
1128–1143 Alfonso Henriques, count of Portugal, makes Portugal independent of Spain and becomes king (to 1185).
1129 Empress Matilda, widow of Henry V, marries Geoffrey Plantagenet (1113–1151) Count of Anjou, in France.
1135 Stephen of Boulogne seizes the English throne on the death of Henry I – rival claims of Matilda causes civil war.
1137–1180 Louis VII, king of France.
1138–1152 Conrad III, Holy Roman emperor.
1139 Matilda lands in England.
1141 Battle of Lincoln – Matilda captures Stephen but after a disastrous, short reign is driven out by popular uprising – Stephen is restored.
1152 Annulment of marriage of Louis VII of France and Eleanor of Aquitaine on grounds of blood relationship. Eleanor marries Henry of Anjou allying Aquitaine with Anjou and Normandy.
1152–1190 Frederick I Barbarossa, Holy Roman emperor.
1153 Henry of Anjou, son of Matilda, invades England and forces Stephen to make him his heir.
1154–1159 Pope Adrian IV (Nicholas Breakspear) – only English pope.
1154–1189 Henry II, king of England – also rules more than half of France.
1155 Henry appoints Thomas à Becket chancellor.
Adrian IV grants Henry II the right to rule Ireland.
1162 Becket is appointed Archbishop of Canterbury – he quarrels with the king over church rights.
1164 Constitutions of Clarendon – set out laws governing the trial of rebellious churchmen in England. Becket flees to France.
1170 Becket, reconciled to Henry II, returns to Canterbury where he is murdered in the cathedral.
1171 Henry II annexes Ireland.
1173 Henry's three eldest sons – Henry, Richard and Geoffrey, supported by Queen Eleanor – rebel.
Canonization of Thomas à Becket.
1180–1223 Philip II, king of France.
1182 Philip banishes Jews from France.
1185–1211 Sancho I, king of Portugal.
1189–1199 Richard I (Coeur de Lion), king of England.
1190–1197 Henry VI, Holy Roman emperor.
1193 Leopold of Austria who had captured Richard I on his return from the Holy Land hands him to the Emperor Henry who demands ransom.
1194 Henry VI captures Sicily.
Richard is ransomed and returns to England.
1197 Civil war in Germany on death of Henry VI.

NEAR EAST

1104 Crusaders capture Acre.
1118–1143 John II Comnenus, Byzantine emperor – a revival of Byzantine power especially in Asia Minor.
1143–1180 Manuel Comnenus, the greatest of the Comneni, continues the Byzantine revival. Constantinople the acknowledged capital of the world and centre of culture.
1147–1149 Second Crusade follows an appeal by St Bernard of Clairvaux to Conrad III and Louis VII – nothing significant achieved.
1169 Saladin, vizier of Egypt – in 1174 he becomes sultan (to 1193).
1174 Saladin conquers Syria.
1177 Baldwin IV of Jerusalem defeats Saladin at Montgisard.
1179 Saladin besieges Tyre.
1180 Truce between Saladin and Baldwin IV.
1180–1183 Alexius II Comnenus, Byzantine emperor.
1183–1185 Andronicus I Comnenus, Byzantine emperor – a reformer, he is deposed and executed. A period of corruption follows.
1185–1195 Isaac II, Byzantine emperor.
1186–1188 Peter and John Asen lead insurrection against Byzantium – the formation of new Bulgarian state.
1187 Saladin captures Jerusalem.
1189–1192 Third Crusade led by Richard of England, Philip of France and Frederick Barbarossa (Holy Roman emperor).
1191 Richard I conquers Cyprus and captures Acre.
1192 Richard captures Jaffa, makes peace with Saladin.
1193 Muslims capture Bihar and Bengal.
1195–1203 Alexius III, Byzantine emperor.

ELSEWHERE

1100 Colonization of the Polynesian islands.
1130–1169 Africa: Almohad dynasty (founded by preacher Ibn Tumat) in power in Morocco.
1145–1150 Africa: Almohads conquer Moorish Spain.
1151 Mexico: End of Toltec empire.
1156–1185 Japan: Civil war.
1161 China: Explosives used at the battle of Ts'ai-shih.
1185–1333 Japan: Kamakura period.
1189 America: Last (known) Norse visit to North America.
1190 Mongols: Temujin begins to create the Mongol empire.
1190–1225 Africa: Lalibela, emperor of Ethiopia.
1192 Japan: Minamoto becomes shogun.
1196–1464 Africa: Marimid dynasty in Morocco – foundation of Fez.

THE CRUSADES

In 1096 Pope Urban 11 appealed for a crusade to free Palestine from the Saracens (Muslims) and the first crusade set out to recover Jerusalem. The most famous crusade was the third (1189–92) led by Richard I (Coeur de Lion) of England, Philip of France and the Emperor Frederick Barbarossa. The leaders quarrelled and Philip returned to France. Richard led his forces within sight of Jerusalem but was unable to take it although Saladin allowed Christians to enter the city under truce. Later crusades were less honourable. In 1212 the Children's Crusade of 50,000 children set off for the Holy Land but most were sold as slaves in Marseilles. The fourth crusade sacked Christian Constantinople. The last crusade was in 1270.

A tile depicting King Richard I of England. He led Crusades to the Holy Land and earned himself the name of Coeur de Lion or Lionheart. Richard's father Henry II had founded a new dynasty – the Angevin. Its popular name is Plantagenet from the sprig of broom *(planta genista)* which Henry's father wore in his cap as a badge.

Below: The routes taken by crusaders on the four main crusades.

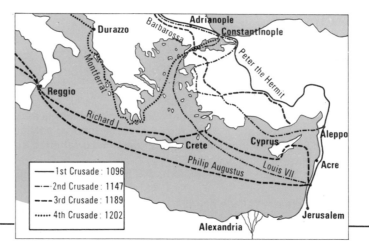

41

THE FEUDAL AGE 1200–1300

EUROPE

1207 Pope Innocent III (1198–1216) appoints Stephen Langton Archbishop of Canterbury. King John does not allow him to take office.

1209 Innocent excommunicates King John.

1210 Innocent excommunicates the emperor Otto IV, Holy Roman Emperor (1198–1212).

1212–1250 Frederick II, Holy Roman Emperor.

1213 Pope Innocent declares King John deposed – John makes peace.

1215 Magna Carta – barons force King John to agree a statement of their rights.

1216–1272 Henry III, king of England at age nine.

1223–1226 Louis VIII, king of France.

1224–1227 War between England and France.

1226–1270 Louis IX (St Louis), king of France.

1227 Henry III begins personal rule without regents in England.

1240 Battle of Neva – Alexander Nevski of Novgorod defeats the Swedes.

1245 Synod of Lyons called by Pope Innocent IV (1243–1254) declares Frederick II deposed.

1247–1250 War in Italy between Frederick and the papal allies.

1250–1254 Conrad IV, Holy Roman emperor.

1254–1273 The Great Interregnum – struggle for the crown of the Holy Roman emperor.

1256 Pope Alexander IV founds the Augustinian Order from several groups of hermits.

Llewellyn ap Griffith drives out the English from Wales.

1264 Simon de Montfort and English barons defeat Henry III at Lewes.

1265 De Montfort parliament – burgesses summoned to parliament from major towns for first time.

Battle of Evesham – de Montfort defeated and killed by Edward (son of Henry III).

1270 Louis IX of France dies on Seventh Crusade.

1270–1285 Philip III, king of France.

1272–1307 Edward I, king of England.

1273–1291 Rudolf I, Holy Roman emperor.

1274 Synod of Lyons – Pope Gregory X (1271–1276) recommends conclaves (meetings) to be secret to avoid corruption.

1279 Rudolf surrenders his claims to Sicily and the papal states.

1283 Edward I completes conquest of Wales. Llewellyn killed in skirmish and his brother David executed.

1285–1314 Philip IV, the Fair, king of France.

1286–1290 Margaret, the 'Maid of Norway' proclaimed queen of Scotland in absence.

1290 Death of Margaret on way to Scotland causes confusion – 13 claimants to Scottish throne.

Edward I expels Jews from England.

1291 Scots accept Edward I as suzerain (nominal controller) – arbitrates in succession dispute.

1292 Edward nominates John Balliol as king of Scotland.

1295 Edward I holds Model Parliament and summons knights and burgesses from shires and towns – the first representative parliament.

1296 Edward I deposes John Balliol of Scotland – who rebelled against the English – interregnum to 1306.

1297 Battle of Cambuskenneth – William Wallace of Scotland defeats English army.

1298 Edward defeats Wallace at Falkirk and reconquers Scotland.

THE MONGOLS

1206 Temujin is proclaimed Genghis Khan – 'Emperor within the Seas'.

1210 Mongols invade China.

1218 Genghis Khan captures Persia.

1219 Mongols conquer Bukhara.

1227 Death of Genghis Khan – empire divided among sons.

1229–1241 Ogadai is elected khan.

1234 Mongols annex the Ch'in empire.

1240 Mongols capture Moscow, destroy Kiev.

1241 Mongols invade Hungary and cross Danube into Austria – they withdraw from Europe on the death of Ogadai.

1242 Batu sets up Mongol kingdom of the 'Golden Horde' on the lower Volga River.

1260 Kublai, Mongol leader, has himself elected khan by his army.

1260–1368 Yuan (Mongol) dynasty in China.

1264 Kublai Khan captures his brother and then reunites the Mongol empire. Transfers capital to Yen-ching and builds Khanbalig (modern Peking).

1268–1279 Mongols obtain control of all China.

1271–1285 Marco Polo, the Venetian traveller (1254–1324), travels to court of Kublai Khan.

1274 Mongol invasion of Japan fails.

1281 Second Mongol invasion of Japan ends in disaster.

1287 Mongols pillage Pagan, capital of Burma.

1289 Friar John of Montecorvino becomes first Archbishop of Peking.

1294 Death of Kublai Khan.

1295–1307 Temur Oljaitu (Ch'eng Tsung) grandson of Kublai Khan is emperor of China – last effective ruler of Yuan dynasty.

1200 Mexico: Hunac Ceel revolts against the Maya of Chichen Itza – he establishes a new capital at Mayapan.
Africa: Jews given special privileges in Morocco.
1202–1204 Fourth Crusade – crusaders unable to pay Venice for transport, capture Constantinople and sack it in order to pay Venetians – instal Latin (Roman) ruler.
1217–1222 Fifth Crusade fails to capture Egypt.
1219–1333 Japan: Hojo Clan rules, after the end of Minamoto family.
1228–1229 Sixth Crusade – crusaders recapture Jerusalem under Emperor Frederick II.
1240 Africa: Old Empire of Ghana is extinguished and incorporated in new kingdom of Mali.
1243 Egyptians capture Jerusalem from the Christians.
1248–1270 Seventh Crusade by Louis IX of France.
1250 Saracens capture Louis IX in Egypt – he is ransomed.
1261–1282 Byzantium: Emperor Michael VIII, restores Byzantine authority.
1290–1320 India: Firuz, Turkish leader, founds the Khalji dynasty in Delhi.
1291 Saracens capture Acre, last Christian stronghold in the Holy Land – this ends period of Crusades.

A 13th-century truckle bed used by servants. When not in use it was stored beneath a larger bed.

A scullion washing dishes in a sink, 1300s. The drain leads to the outside of the castle.

Left: A Medieval carpenter.

Right: The first spinning wheels were invented in the 13th century.

A bench used in a refectory (a monastic dining hall) and a crude bench with a back, 13th century.

THE FEUDAL SYSTEM

Feudalism provided a structure for medieval Europe which lasted several centuries. The ruler (King or Emperor) granted land to his greatest followers in return for their loyalty and military service. In turn these great barons granted smaller estates to their vassals who owed allegiance to their lord and through him to the king. At the bottom of the scale came freemen and serfs: the freemen had some liberties, the serfs almost none. Everyone owed a duty to someone above him.

king   bishop   baron   knights   yeoman   serf

THE FEUDAL AGE 1300–1400

EUROPE

1301 Edward I invests his son, Edward, as Prince of Wales.
1302 Battle of Courtrai – Flemish burghers defeat French knights and prevent occupation by France.
1305 Execution of Scottish patriot, William Wallace, by English.
1305–1377 Papal See moved to Avignon.
1306 Philip IV expels Jews from France.
Robert Bruce leads Scottish rebellion against English – crowned at Scone.
1307–1327 Edward II, king of England.
1314 Battle of Bannockburn – Robert Bruce defeats the weak Edward II and makes Scotland independent.
1316–1334 John XXII Pope.
1317 France adopts Salic law which excludes women from succession to the throne.
1326 Queen Isabella and Roger Mortimer sail from France with an army to rebel against Edward II of England.
1327 Parliament declares Edward II deposed – Edward III succeeds his father. Edward II is murdered.
Louis IV, Holy Roman emperor (1314–1347), invades Italy and declares Pope John XXII deposed.
1328–1350 Philip VI, king of France founds House of Valois.
1333 Edward III defeats Scots, who had rebelled at Halidon Hill.
1337 Edward III, provoked by attacks on his French territories, declares himself King of France – the beginning of the '100 Years War'.
1340 Battle of Sluys – English defeat French and gain control of the Channel.
English parliament passes statutes that taxation may only be imposed by parliament.
1346 Edward III invades France and defeats French at Crécy.
1347 English capture Calais.
1349 Persecution of Jews in Germany.
1353 Statute of Praemunire – English parliament forbids appeals to the pope.
1356 Battle of Poitiers – Edward the Black Prince, son of Edward III, defeats the French and captures King John II.
1358 Jacquerie revolt by French peasants is suppressed by the regent Charles, son of John II.
1360 Treaty of Brétigny ends the first stage of the '100 Years War' – Edward III gives up his claim to the French throne.
1369 Renewed war between France and England.
1371 Robert II, king of Scotland – the first Stuart monarch.
1372 French recapture Poitou and Brittany from English.
1374 John of Gaunt, son of Edward III, rules England – the king is too old and the Black Prince is ill.
1377 Pope Gregory XI returns to Rome.
1377–1399 Richard II, king of England on death of Edward III.
1381 Peasants' Revolt in England.
1382 Scots with a French army attack England.
1389 Truce halts fighting between English, French and Scots until 1396.
1397 Union of Kalmar brings Norway, Denmark and Sweden under one King, Eric of Pomerania.
1399 Henry Bolingbroke, on death of John of Gaunt, his father, deposes Richard II to become Henry IV, king of England.

NEAR EAST & THE OTTOMANS

1290–1326 Osman I, founder of the Ottoman dynasty based on the Black Sea coast of Asia Minor.
1301 Osman defeats the Byzantines.
1326 Bursa becomes Ottoman capital.
1326–1359 Orkhan I – first clear ruler and organizer of Ottoman Turks.
1345 Ottomans first cross the Bosporus into Europe.
1369–1372 Ottomans conquer Bulgaria.
1371 Ottomans defeat Serbs, and conquer Macedonia.
1389 Battle of Kossovo – Ottomans defeat a coalition of Serbs, Bulgars, Bosnians, Wallachians and Albanians.
1390 Ottomans complete the conquest of Asia Minor.
1391–1398 First siege of Constantinople by Turks. Constantinople pays tribute.
1396 Abortive crusade by about 20,000 European knights against Turks – defeated at Nicopolis.
1397 Turks invade Greece.

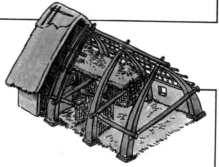

To train for war in the 1400s knights fought in mock battles. This was called jousting.

In the 1300s timber-framed houses were built for animals and their owners. The animals lived at one end.

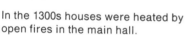

In the 1300s houses were heated by open fires in the main hall.

An early type of cannon as used at Crécy in 1346.

Salisbury cathedral clock mechanism, 1386. This is one of the very first clocks.

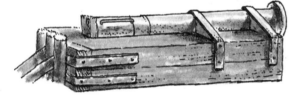

THE BLACK DEATH

One of the greatest plagues in history the Black Death originated in China and was carried along trade routes to Europe by fleas on rats. It reached Cyprus in 1347 and then swept across Europe (1348). About 25 million people in Europe (half the population) died. The results of this devastation was a new economic order. A desperate shortage of labour meant that wages rose by 50 per cent or more. This shortage of labour and land left untenanted by the dead meant that humble people became more important. This helped end the feudal system.

EUROPE

1400 Richard II murdered. Owen Glendower leads rebellion of the Welsh.
1402 Henry IV invades Wales.
1405 French land in Wales to support Glendower.
1406 Henry, Prince of Wales, defeats Welsh.
1406–1437 James I, king of Scotland, (captive in England 1406–1423).
1409 Gregory XII pope in Rome (to 1415). Benedict XIII – anti-pope based at Avignon – recognized by France, Scotland and parts of Germany and Italy. Council of Pisa called to resolve the Great Schism. Deposes the rival popes and elects a third – Alexander V – anti-pope at Pisa. All the popes refuse to resign. The schism is now a triple one.
1410–1415 John XXIII, anti-pope at Pisa.
1414–1417 Council of Constance, called by Pope John XXIII, deposes John, persuades Gregory to resign and isolates Benedict XIII.
1415 Henry V revives English claim to French throne and invades France – defeats French at Agincourt.
1417–1431 Pope Martin V – end of Great Schism.
1419 Henry allies with Philip II of Burgundy (Burgundy is independent from France).
1420 Treaty of Troyes – Henry V acknowledged heir to the French throne by the insane French king, Charles VI. Henry marries Catherine, daughter of Charles VI.
1422 Death of Henry V and Charles VI – War flares up again.
1422–1461 Infant Henry VI, king of England.
Charles VII, king of France (Dauphin to 1429).
1424 Battle of Cravant – Duke of Bedford (regent) defeats the French. Last of the great English victories in '100 Years War'.
1428 English besiege Orléans.
1429 Joan of Arc, in command of French forces, raises the siege of Orléans.
1430 Burgundians capture Joan of Arc and hand her over to the English.
1431 Joan of Arc is burnt at Rouen, Burgundy, as a witch.
Henry VI of England crowned king of France in Paris under treaty.
1434 Cosimo Medici becomes ruler of Florence.
1436 English troops withdraw from Paris.
1439 Council of Basle deposes Pope Eugene IV – Felix V anti-pope to 1449.
1451 Birth of Christopher Columbus, dies 1506.
1451–1453 England swept from France. Only Calais is retained by English. End of '100 Years War' between France and England.

ELSEWHERE

1401 Tamerlane takes Damascus and Baghdad.
1402 Battle of Angora – Bayazid, the Turkish sultan, defeated and captured by Tamerlane. He overruns most of the Ottoman empire which saves Byzantium.
1403 Tamerlane withdraws from Anatolia.
1403–1433 China sends a series of naval expeditions through the south seas as far as Sumatra, Ceylon, Hormuz, Aden.
1404–1447 Shah Rukh (fourth son of Tamerlane) rules Persia.
1405 Death of Tamerlane on way to China to convert them to Islam. Mongol empire disintegrates.
1405–1413 Civil war in Ottoman empire.
1411–1442 Ahmad Shah in western India builds Ahmadabad as his capital – it becomes one of most beautiful cities in world.
1413–1421 Muhammad I consolidates Ottoman power.
1421–1451 Sultan Murad II – rivalry between Ottomans and Venice.
1433 Africa: Tuaregs from Sahara sack Timbuktu.
1438 S. America: Inca empire established in Peru.
1442 S. America: Portuguese find gold at Rio de Oro.
1444 W. Africa: Huno Tristan reaches the Senegal River – the first green coastline (not desert).
1444 Second western crusade against the Turks is crushed at Varna.
1451–1481 Muhammad II, sultan of Turkey.
1453 The fall of Constantinople to the Turks after a siege of 54 days marks the end of the Byzantine empire and is usually regarded as the end of the Middle Ages.

JOAN OF ARC

The 100 Years War between England and France (1336–1453) was the last great struggle of the feudal era. At the siege of Paris (1430) a young peasant girl claimed to hear voices telling her to approach the uncrowned king of France and demand to lead his forces in battle. She inspired the French but was captured by the Burgundians who handed her over to the English. They burnt her as a witch; she became a martyr and saint.

NEW HORIZONS 1453–1650

The two centuries (1453–1650) were a period of rapid change. They saw the end of feudalism and the spread of new learning (the Renaissance) helped by the invention of printing which affected every aspect of life. This was the period when the powers of Europe, led by Spain and Portugal, began to expand overseas and colonize the New World.

Florence, one of the richest cities in northern Italy, was the birthplace of the Renaissance.

EUROPE & AMERICA

1455–1485 Wars of the Roses in England.
1467 Charles the Bold, duke of Burgundy.
1469 Unification of Spain follows the marriage of Ferdinand of Aragon and Isabella of Castile.
1485 Battle of Bosworth – Henry VII founds Tudor dynasty in England.
1492 Spain conquers Granada and ends Muslim influence in the Iberian peninsula.
Christopher Columbus crosses Atlantic and discovers the West Indies.
1493 Pope divides New World between Spain and Portugal.
1497 John Cabot discovers Newfoundland.
1500 Pedro Cabral claims Brazil for Portugal.
1501 Negro slaves introduced to the Spanish Indies.
France and Spain occupy Naples.
1511–1515 Spanish conquer Cuba.
1518 Cortes begins conquest of Mexico (Aztecs).
1519–1556 Charles V, Holy Roman emperor.
1529 Peace of Cambrai between France and Spain – France renounces her claims to Italy.
1533 Pizarro captures Cuzco – collapse of Inca empire.

Prince Henry the Navigator of Portugal (1394–1460) sent a series of expeditions down the western coast of Africa. He also built an observatory and founded a school of navigation.

ELSEWHERE

1456 Ottomans: Turks capture Athens.
1467 Japan: Start of civil wars.
1468 Africa: Sunni Ali takes Timbuktu from Tuaregs – rise of Songhay empire.
1472 Ottomans: Turks defeat Persians at battle of Otlukbeli.
1475 Ottomans: Turks conquer Crimea.
1514 Ottomans: War between Turkey and Persia – the beginning of a long duel.
1517 Ottomans: Turks capture Cairo – end of Mameluke empire.
1526 Mongols: Battle of Panipat – Babar the Mongol defeats sultan of Delhi and founds Mughal empire in north India.
1534 Ottomans: Turks capture Tunis, Baghdad and Mesopotamia from Persia.

Leonardo da Vinci (right) was one of the most talented people of the Renaissance. He was an artist, architect, engineer, inventor, astronomer and mathematician.

Below: Leonardo's design for a multi-barrelled gun.

A detail from Leonardo's painting *Virgin and St Anne*.

CULTURE & RELIGION

1453 Turks convert basilica of St Sophia, Constantinople into a mosque.
1454 Gutenberg prints his first bible.
1465 First printed music.
1466–1536 Erasmus of Rotterdam, Dutch scholar regarded as leader of learning in Renaissance in northern Europe.
1475–1564 Michelangelo Buonarotti, Italian artist.
1477 William Caxton prints Chaucer's *Canterbury Tales*.
1477–1576 Titian, Italian painter.
1478–1535 Thomas More, English Catholic humanist.
1483–1520 Raphael, Italian painter.
1484 Botticelli (1444–1510) paints his *Birth of Venus*.
1492 By order of the Spanish inquisitor, Torquemada, Jews are given three months to accept Christianity or leave the country.
1492–1556 Pietro Aretino, Italian author and satirist.
1494 Italian preacher, Girolamo Savonarola, holds power in Florence until 1497 when burned at the stake.
1494–1553 François Rabelais, French writer.
1503 Leonardo's *Mona Lisa*.
1508–1512 Michelangelo paints Sistine Chapel ceiling.
1517 Luther at Wittenberg sets off the Reformation.
1521 Diet of Worms – Martin Luther (1483–1546) is condemned as a heretic by Rome and excommunicated.
1532 John Calvin starts Protestant movement in France.
Religious Peace of Nuremburg – Protestants allowed to practise their religion freely.
1534 Act of Supremacy in England makes Henry VIII supreme head of the English Church.
Ignatius Loyola founds Jesuits.

DEVELOPMENTS

1464 Louis XI establishes imperial mail service.
1473–1543 Nicolaus Copernicus, European astronomer, who first stated that the earth and other planets turn around the sun.
1488 Bartholomew Diaz rounds Cape of Good Hope.
1489 Symbols + (plus) and − (minus) come into use.
1492 First globe constructed by Nuremberg geographer, Martin Beheim (1459–1507).
1498 Modern toothbrush first described in Chinese encyclopedia.
Vasco da Gama reaches India.
1501 Amerigo Vespucci explores coast of Brazil.
1502 Peter Henlein of Nuremberg constructs the first watch.
1503 Pocket handkerchief comes into use.
1503–1566 Nostradamus, French astrologer.
1507 Waldseemuller's map shows South America separate from Asia, proposes the New World be called America after Amerigo Vespucci.
1510–1590 Ambroise Paré, French surgeon – one of the greatest of all time.
1513 Vasco Nuñez de Balboa discovers Pacific Ocean.
1517 Coffee in Europe for the first time.
1520 Chocolate brought from Mexico to Spain.
1521 Manufacture of silk introduced to France.
1522 First circumnavigation of the world by Magellan's expedition.
1533 First lunatic asylums.
1535 First diving bells.

Johannes Gutenberg, inventor of printing from movable metal type, checking a printed sheet.

EUROPE & AMERICA

1547 Ivan IV (The Terrible) is crowned tsar of Russia.
1548 Charles V annexes the Netherlands to the Holy Roman Empire.
1555 Peace of Augsburg allows Protestant princes freedom of worship in Holy Roman empire.
1562 John Hawkins starts English slave trade from west Africa to the Indies.
1568 Netherlands revolt against Spain.
1571 Battle of Lepanto – Papal-Venetian fleet defeats Turks.
1580 Spain conquers Portugal.
1581 Union of Utrecht.
1584 Raleigh founds a colony in Virginia.
1588 Spanish Armada against England is defeated.
1598 Edict of Nantes ends religious wars in France.
1607 John Smith founds English colony at Jamestown, Virginia.
1618 Defenestration of Prague leads to the Thirty Years War.
1620 *Mayflower* reaches Cape Cod – New Plymouth (later Boston) is founded.
1624–1642 Richelieu first minister of France.
1626 Dutch found New Amsterdam (later New York).
1628 Petition of Right – Charles I accepts statement of civil rights in return for funds.
1632 Battle of Lützen – death of Gustavus Adolphus of Sweden.
1640 Portuguese revolt against Spain.
1642 French found Montreal.
1642–1646 Civil war in England.
1648 Treaty of Westphalia ends the Thirty Years War – Holland and Switzerland to be independent.
1649 Execution of Charles I.
Commonwealth in England.

ELSEWHERE

1541 Ottomans: Turks conquer Hungary.
1557 Portuguese establish a settlement at Macao in China.
1570 Japan: Nagasaki opened to foreign trade.
1573 Venice abandons Cyprus.
1577 India: Akbar the Great, Mughal emperor, unifies north India.
1590 Hideyoshi unifies Japan.
1591 Africa: Moroccans defeat army of Songhay empire which then disintegrates.
1593 Japanese withdraw from Korea after invading it in 1592.
1595 Japan: Dutch settle on Guinea coast.
1600 Japan: Tokugawa period.
India: English East India Company founded.
1603 Japan: Shogun Ieyasu.
1604 India: French East India Company founded..
Russians settle Siberia.
1638 Japan: Slaughter of Japanese Christians.
1644 China: Manchu dynasty founded.
1645 Ottomans: Turks and Venice at war over Crete.

From the cliffs and shores of England people watched in amazement as the Spanish Armada sailed up the Channel.

CULTURE & RELIGION

1541 Knox brings the Reformation to Scotland.
1545 Council of Trent opened by Pope Paul III to reform Catholic Church under Jesuit guidance.
St Francis Xavier introduces Christianity to Japan.
1547–1616 Miguel de Cervantes, Spanish writer.
1549 Book of Common Prayer in England.
1555 England returns to Catholicism under Mary.
1561–1626 Francis Bacon, English philosopher and statesman.
1563 39 Articles set out agreed beliefs of Church of England.
1564–1616 William Shakespeare.
1566 *Notizie Scritte*, one of first newspapers, in Venice.
1572 Mass murder of Protestants (Huguenots) in France on St Bartholomew's Day.
1573–1652 Inigo Jones, English architect.
1577–1640 Peter Paul Rubens, Flemish painter.
1586 Beginning of Japanese Kabuki theatre.
1592 Pompeii ruins discovered.
1593–1665 Nicholas Poussin, French painter.
1596–1650 René Descartes, French philosopher.
1598 Edict of Nantes allows Huguenots equal rights with Catholics in France.
1606–1669 Rembrandt van Rijn, Dutch painter.
1611 King James' Authorized Version of the Bible.
1618–1648 Thirty Years War devastates central Europe.
1621–1695 Jean de la Fontaine, French poet.
1622–1673 Jean-Baptiste Molière, French dramatist.
1628–1650 Taj Mahal built in Agra, India.
1629 Shah Jahan, the Great Moghul, orders the making of the Peacock Throne.
1632–1723 Christopher Wren, English architect.
1639–1699 Racine, French dramatist.
1642 Abel Tasman, Dutch mariner, discovers Van Diemen's Land (now Tasmania).

Japanese mounted warriors – samurai – were only defeated when firearms were introduced in 1542.

DEVELOPMENTS

1553 Tobacco brought from America to Spain.
1554–1618 Sir Walter Raleigh, English explorer, author and courtier.
1562 Milled coins introduced in England to counteract clipping.
1564–1642 Galileo Galilei, great Italian scientist.
1565 First graphite pencil described by Swiss, Konrad Gaesner.
1577 Francis Drake sails round the world.
1585 Antwerp loses its importance as international port to Rotterdam and Amsterdam.
1589 Knitting machine invented by Englishman, William Lee.
Water closet installed by Sir John Harington at his home.
1596 Galileo invents thermometer.
1598 Korean admiral Vesunsin invents iron-clad warship.
1600 Dutch opticians invent the telescope.
1606 Willem Jansz sights Australia.
Galileo invents proportional compass.
1609 Keppler's laws of planetary motion.
1610 Thomas Harriett discovers sunspots.
1619 William Harvey announces his discovery of the circulation of the blood.
1624 Submarine consisting of skin of greased leather over a wooden frame, made by Dutchman, Cornelius Drebbel.
1630 Beginning of public advertising in Paris.
1635 Sale of tobacco in France restricted to apothecaries – only on doctor's prescription.
1637 First umbrella known, in France.
1638 Torture abolished in England.
1639 First printing press in N. America at Cambridge, Mass.
1642 Income and property tax introduced in England.
1643 Italian physicist Torricelli invents the barometer.
1650 World population estimated at 500 million.

EUROPE

1455–1485 Wars of the Roses in England between the royal houses of York (Richard) and Lancaster (Henry VI).
Battle of Roxburgh – James II of Scotland killed, James III reigns to 1488.
1461 Edward of York defeats the Lancastrians to become Edward IV – to 1483.
1462 Castile captures Gibraltar from Arabs.
1462–1505 Ivan III (the Great), Duke of Moscow, laid the foundations of the Russian empire.
1466 Peace of Thorn – Poland gains large area of Prussia from the Teutonic Knights.
1467 Charles the Bold becomes duke of Burgundy – main rival to Louis XI of France.
1469 Marriage of Ferdinand of Aragon and Isabella of Castile ensures future unification of Spain.
1470 Warwick turns Lancastrian, defeats Edward IV and restores Henry VI.
1471 Battle of Barnet – Edward IV defeats and kills Warwick; Henry VI dies in the Tower (probably murdered).
1474 War between Louis XI and Charles the Bold (now allied to Edward IV).
Isabella succeeds to the throne of Castile.
1474–1477 Charles the Bold of Burgundy at war with the Swiss Federation, who objects to Charles attempting to extend his lands.
1476 William Caxton sets up his printing press at Westminster.
1477 Battle of Nancy – Charles the Bold is defeated and killed by the Swiss.
1478 Ferdinand and Isabella establish the Spanish Inquisition with consent of Pope Sixtus IV (1471–1484). Its main aim is to punish so-called converted Jews who still practise their old faith in secret.
Ivan III incorporates Novgorod into duchy of Moscow.
Hungary gains Moravia and Silesia.
1478–1492 Lorenzo de Medici rules Florence.
1479 Spain formally united by union of Aragon and Castile – Ferdinand V of Castile, king of Aragon to 1516.
1483 Death of Edward IV – Richard of Gloucester deposes Edward V to become Richard III. Edward V and his brother are murdered in the Tower, but when and by whom is uncertain.
1485 Battle of Bosworth – Henry Tudor, Earl of Richmond defeats and kills Richard III. He becomes Henry VII, king of England and first of the Tudor monarchs.
Hungary takes Vienna and lower Austria to become most powerful state in central Europe.
1488–1513 James IV, king of Scotland.
1494 Charles VIII of France (1483–1498) invades Italy.
1498 Florentine preacher and brief ruler, Savonarola burned at stake.
1499 Louis XII of France (1498–1515) invades Italy.
1500 Louis XII conquers Milan. Treaty of Granada – Louis and Ferdinand V agree to divide Naples.

ELSEWHERE

1449–1490 Japan: Rule of Shogun Yoshimasa – period of creative art.
1453–1478 Persia: Uzun Hasan – period of expansion; ally of Venice.
1456 Ottoman Turks capture Athens.
1459 Turks conquer Serbia.
1460 Turks conquer Morea.
1461 Turks conquer Trebizond – the last ancient Greek state.
1463–1479 War between Turkey and Venice.
1464–1492 Africa: Sunni Ali rules Songhay empire in west Africa.
1467 Japan: Beginning of 100 years of civil wars.
Africa: Sunni Ali of Songhay recaptures Timbuktu from Tuaregs.
1470 Turks take Negroponte from the Venetians.
1471 Africa: Portuguese seize Tangier from Muslims.
1472 Venetians destroy Ottoman town of Smyrna.
Battle of Otlukbeli – Turks defeat Persians, the chief allies of the Venetians.
1473 Persia: Uzun Hasan of Persia defeated by Turks at Ersindjam.
1475 Turks conquer Crimea.
1478 Turks conquer Albania.
1478–1490 Persia: Jaqub rules – a period of enlightened rule.
1479 Treaty of Constantinople ends war between Turkey and Venice. Venice agrees to pay tribute to Turks for trading rights in Black Sea.
1480 Turks occupy Otranto in southern Italy.
1493 Africa: Songhay empire reaches its height, absorbs much of Mandingo empire.

EXPLORATION

1450s Great impetus to exploration was trade. Overland trade too expensive, so alternative routes sought.
1455–1456 Cadamosto, Venetian sailor explores the Senegal and Gambia rivers and discovers Cape Verde Islands.
1472 Portuguese discover Fernando Po, an island off present day Cameroun in Africa.
1482–1484 Portuguese navigator, Diego Cao explores the Congo River.
Portuguese settlement on Gold Coast (Ghana).
1487 Portuguese reach Timbuktu overland from coast.
1488 Diaz rounds Cape of Good Hope.
1490 Portuguese ascend River Congo, about 200 miles, 'convert' king of Congo to Christianity.
1492 Genoan-born Christopher Columbus makes first landfall in West Indies – Cuba – on behalf of Spain.
1493 Pope Alexander VI divides New World between Spain and Portugal.
1497 Italian explorer John Cabot discovers Newfoundland.
1498 Vasco da Gama of Portugal reaches India. Columbus discovers Trinidad and South America.
1500 Pedro Cabral claims Brazil for Portugal.

DISCOVERING AMERICA

In 1492 a Genoese navigator, Christopher Columbus (1451–1506), sailed west to find the Indies. He landed on Cuba, the largest island of the group we now call the West Indies. He did not realize that a whole continent lay between him and the Indies. Amerigo Vespucci reported this in 1502 and the Americas are named after him. The discovery of the Americas showed the world to be far larger than anyone had imagined. For the next three centuries the two large land masses of North and South America – as well as the West Indian islands – became the objects of European imperial rivalries as Spanish, Portuguese, Dutch, English and French empires were established from Hudson's Bay to the Falklands.

Ivan the Third, known as 'the Great' laid the foundations of the Russian empire.

Vasco da Gama, the Portuguese navigator, was the first person to sail to India from Europe around the Cape of Good Hope.

EUROPE

1501 France and Spain occupy Naples.
1501–1503 Russia and Poland at War – Russia gains Lithuania and other border territories.
1503 Spain defeats France at the battles of Cerignola and Garigliano.
1505 Treaty of Blois – France keeps Milan but cedes Naples to Spain which now controls all southern Italy.
1509–1547 Henry VIII, king of England.
1512–1520 Selim I, sultan of Turkey.
1512–1522 Russia and Poland at War.
1513 Battle of Novara – French driven from Italy.
Battle of Flodden Field – James IV of Scotland killed by English; James V king to 1542.
1515 Thomas Wolsey, Archbishop of York is made Lord Chancellor of England and a cardinal.
1515–1547 François I, king of France.
Battle of Marignano – French defeat Swiss and regain Milan.
1516–1556 Charles I, king of Spain.
1519 Charles I becomes Charles V, Holy Roman emperor.
1520 Field of Cloth of Gold at Calais – meeting of Henry VIII and François I fails to gain Henry's support against Charles V. Henry VIII makes secret treaty with Charles V.
1520–1566 Suleiman I, sultan of Turkey – empire at its height in his reign.
1521 Ottoman Turks capture Belgrade.
1521–1529 France and Spain at war again over Italy.
1522 Battle of Biocca – Charles V drives French from Milan.
1524 France invades Italy – retakes Milan.
1525 Battle of Pavia – François I is captured.
1526 Treaty of Madrid – François I gives up claim to Milan, Genoa, Naples; subsequently does not keep treaty.
Battle of Mohacs – Turks defeat and kill Louis II of Bohemia and Hungary.
League of Cognac formed against Charles V by François I, Pope Clement VII, Milan, Florence and Venice.
1527 Spanish and German mercenary troops sack Rome – Pope Clement VII is captured.
1529 Peace of Cambrai between France and Spain – France renounces claims to Italy.
1532 Turks invade Hungary but are defeated.
1533 Peace between Turkey and Austria.
1536 Anne Boleyn executed – Henry VIII marries Jane Seymour. She dies after the birth of a son in 1537.
France invades Savoy and Piedmont in Italy.
1540 Henry VIII marries Anne of Cleves (arranged by Thomas Cromwell), divorces her and marries Catherine Howard. Cromwell executed for treason.
1542 Catherine Howard is executed.
Battle of Solway Moss – James V of Scotland killed by English, Mary Stuart, queen of Scotland to 1567.
1543 Alliance of Henry VIII and Charles V against France and Scotland.
1547 Death of Henry VIII – Edward VI, king of England to 1553.
Ivan IV (the Terrible) is crowned tsar (emperor) of Russia.
1547–1559 Henri II, king of France.
1548 Charles V annexes the Netherlands.
1548–1572 Sigismund II, king of Poland.

REFORMATION

1517 Martin Luther, Augustinian monk, nails his 95 Theses (reasons) challenging the sale of indulgences (pardons for sins), to the door of the church in Wittenberg.
1521 Diet of Worms – Luther is condemned as a heretic and excommunicated by the pope.
1529 Henry VIII dismisses Cardinal Wolsey (Lord Chancellor) for his failure to obtain the pope's consent to his divorce from Catherine of Aragon.
Sir Thomas More appointed Lord Chancellor.
1530 Civil war in Switzerland between Roman Catholic and Protestant cantons.
1532 Religious Peace of Nuremberg – Protestants allowed to practise their own religion.
John Calvin starts Protestant movement in France.
1533 Henry VIII marries Anne Boleyn and is excommunicated by the pope.
1534 Act of Supremacy – Henry VIII declared supreme head of Church of England.
Ignatius Loyola founds the Society of Jesus (Jesuits).
1535 Sir Thomas More executed for failing to take Oath of Supremacy.
1536 Calvin leads Protestants in Geneva.
Thomas Cromwell supervises the suppression of the monasteries in England – to 1539.
Catholic uprising in the north of England – The Pilgrimage of Grace – suppressed.
1541 John Knox brings the Reformation to Scotland.
1545 Council of Trent opened, which, under Jesuit guidance, is to reform the Catholic Church.
1549 Book of Common Prayer in England brings uniform Protestant services.

HOME LIFE

A German aristocrat and his wife, 1557. Both costumes closely follow Spanish fashions of the time.

An English town house of the 1500s. The timberwork has been carved to look like the stern of a galleon.

Left: Italian folding armchair and a chair in the house of a merchant.

A Norwegian house made of spruce timber, 1500. The roof is covered with turf as insulation and water-proofing.

THE REFORMATION

Until the 16th century Europe had for a thousand years accepted one form of Christianity with the Pope in Rome as the head of the Church. The new learning of the Renaissance added to the doubts which already existed about Church teaching. In 1517 Martin Luther nailed a famous protest against indulgences (pardons for sins which could be purchased) to the door of the church of Wittenberg. This protest set off the Reformation. Calvin in France and Knox in Scotland began similar protests at the way the Church was run. Those who opposed the old ways became known as Protestants. One result was that services (as well as Bibles and prayer books) were translated from Latin into the common languages of Europe. The Reformation sparked off nearly two centuries of bitter struggles between Catholics and Protestants.

EXPLORATION & IMPERIALISM

1501–1502 Amerigo Vespucci explores the coast of Brasil.
1502 Columbus discovers Nicaragua.
1502–1524 Shah Ismail founds the Safavid dynasty in Persia.
1505 Francisco de Almeida sent out as first Portuguese governor of India.
1506 Africa: Portuguese settlements in Mozambique.
1509 Almeida destroys a Muslim fleet at the battle of Diu and gains control of Indian seas.
1513 Portuguese reach Canton, China.
Vasco Nuñez de Balboa crosses Panama isthmus to sight Pacific.
Africa: Portuguese ascend the Zambezi River and establish posts at Sena and Tete.
1518 Hernan Cortes begins conquest of Mexico.
1519 Ferdinand Magellan begins circumnavigation of the globe – dies en route, 1521.
1521 Cortes captures Aztec capital, Tenochtitlan and soon ends Aztec power. Mexico City erected on site of Tenochtitlan.
1522 One of Magellan's ships completes the first circumnavigation of the world.
1522–1533 Spanish exploration of Pacific coast of South America under Francisco Pizarro.
1533 Pizarro captures the Inca capital, Cuzco and conquers Peru.
1535–1536 Jacques Cartier navigates the St Lawrence River in Canada.
1541 Hernando de Soto discovers the Mississippi.
1546–1550 Emperor Charles V, fearful of a separatist movement among the Spanish colonies of South America, appoints Pedro de la Gasca as governor who unites them.

EUROPE & AMERICA

1553 Death of Edward VI – Duke of Northumberland, the Lord Protector, proclaims Lady Jane Grey queen for 9 days.
Mary I is queen until 1558 – restores Catholic bishops.
1554 Execution of Lady Jane Grey.
Mary marries Philip, heir to the throne of Spain.
1555 England returns to Catholicism – about 300 Protestants, including Cranmer, burnt at stake.
Peace of Augsburg – Protestant princes in Holy Roman empire allowed freedom of worship.
1556 Abdication of Charles V.
Philip II, king of Spain, its colonies, the Netherlands and Italian possessions.
Ferdinand (brother to Charles) becomes emperor and ruler of Habsburg lands.
1558 England loses Calais – its last possession in France.
1558–1603 Elizabeth I, queen of England, repeals Catholic legislation.
1560 Treaty of Edinburgh between England, Scotland and France.
Charles IX, king of France to 1574.
1562–1568 John Hawkins takes cargoes of slaves from west Africa to Hispaniola.
1563 39 Articles complete establishment of Church of England.
1565 Portuguese attack French settlement in South America and then found Rio de Janeiro (1567).
1567 Murder of Lord Darnley (husband of Mary, Queen of Scots) probably by Earl of Bothwell whom the queen at once marries. She is imprisoned and forced to abdicate.
1567–1625 James VI, king of Scotland.
1568 Mary Queen of Scots flees to England and is imprisoned by Queen Elizabeth.
1572 Massacre of 20,000 Huguenots in France on St Bartholomew's day.
1576 Pacification of Ghent – the Netherland provinces unite to drive out the Spanish.
Protestantism forbidden in France.
1578 Duke of Parma of Spain subdues southern provinces of Netherlands.
1579 Union of Utrecht formed by northern provinces of Netherlands.
1580 Spain conquers Portugal.
1581 Union of Utrecht declares itself the Dutch Republic – elects William (the Silent) of Orange as ruler.
1584 Murder of William of Orange – England aids Netherlands.
1585–1589 War of three Henrys in France: Henry III (Catholic), Henri of Guise (Holy Catholic League) and Henri of Navarre (Protestant).
1587 Execution of Mary Queen of Scots. England at war with Spain – Drake destroys Spanish fleet at Cadiz.
1588 Spanish Armada against England.
Henri de Guise is murdered.
1589 Murder of Henri III – Henri of Navarre becomes king of France as Henry IV – to 1610.
1590 Henri IV defeats French Catholics at battle of Ivry.
1597–1601 Irish rebellion under Hugh O'Neill, Earl of Tyrone.
1598 Edict of Nantes ends civil war in France – gives Huguenots equal rights with Catholics.
1599 Defeat of Earl of Essex by Irish rebels in Ireland.

ASIA

1551–1562 War between Turkey and Hungary.
1552 Russians begin expansion into Asia.
1554–1556 Turks conquer north African coast.
1556 Battle of Panipat – Akbar the Great defeats the Hindus.
1556–1606 Akbar consolidates the Mughal empire in north India.
1566 Death of Suleiman – the Turkish empire now at its greatest extent.
1566–1574 Selim II, sultan of Turkey.
1570 Turks attack Cyprus.
1571 Battle of Lepanto – Turkish fleet under Ali Pasha destroyed by Don John of Austria and Papal-Venetian fleet.
1573 Venice abandons Cyprus and makes peace with Turkey. Don John recaptures Tunis from Turks.
1574 Turkey regains Tunis from Spain and ravages coasts of western Mediterranean despite the defeat of Lepanto.
1577 Akbar completes the unification and annexation of northern India.
1581 Peace between Turkey and Spain – confirmed in 1585.
1585 Start of decline of Turkish empire, rise of the Janissaries (Turkish soldiers).
1587–1629 Shah Abbas I, the Great, of Persia – period of Persian greatness after decline.
1590 Abbas of Persia makes peace with Turkey – Turkish frontiers now on the Caucasus and Caspian.
1592 Akbar conquers Sind.
1593–1606 Turkey at war with Austria.
1596 Battle of Keresztes – Turks defeat Hungarians.

ELSEWHERE

1557 China: Portuguese establish a settlement at Macao.

1568–1600 Japan: Period of national unification – revival after civil wars.

1570 Japan: Nagasaki opened to foreign trade – Japan's greatest port.

1571–1603 Africa: Bornu empire (Sudan) reaches greatest extent under Idris.

1574 Africa: Portuguese begin to settle the coast of Angola.

1577 So-nam gya-tso reforms Tibetan Buddhism – becomes Dalai Lama.

1578 Africa: Battle of Al Kasr Al-kabil – the Portuguese are defeated by Muslims in Morocco.
Ahmed al Mansur establishes the Sharifian dynasty in Morocco.

1581 Moroccans begin penetration of Sahara.

1583 Sir Humphrey Gilbert takes possession of Newfoundland for England.

1591 Moroccans aided by Portuguese and Spanish mercenaries defeat forces of the Songhay empire which then disintegrates.

1592 Japan under Hideyoshi invades Korea – plans attack on China.

1595 Africa: Dutch settle on the Guinea coast.

1598 Dutch take Mauritius, off south-east coast of Africa.

1600 Battle of Sekigahara – Tokugawa Ieyasu defeats rivals and becomes ruler of Japan. He establishes his headquarters at Edo (Tokyo).

NEWS AND ENTERTAINMENT

Town criers made public announcements and were important in Europe in the 16th century before newspapers.

Kabuki theatre dates back to 1586 and remains the principal form of drama in Japan. The stage is always the same shape.

Religious plays known as Miracles and Mysteries were at first performed in churches. Later they were put on at pageants out of doors.

An early newspaper – *The Antwerp Gazette* of 17 June 1621. It reports with a picture the continuing struggle of what we now call the Thirty Years War.

Commedia dell'arte was popular mime and improvisation in Italy in the 16th century. The main characters were Gilles, Columbine and Harlequin.

A pump used to drain mines, 1500s.

Shakespeare's Globe Theatre. The stage was on two levels.

EUROPE

1603–1625 James VI of Scotland becomes James I of England. He believes in the 'Divine Right of Kings'.

1605 Failure of 'Gunpowder Plot' to blow up House of Lords during James I's state opening of parliament.

1608 Formation of Protestant Union in Germany – led by Frederick IV.

1609 Formation of Catholic League – led by Maximilian of Bavaria.

1610 Assassination of Henry IV, king of France.

1614 Estates-General summoned in France by Maria, queen regent of France, to curb power of nobility.

1618 'Defenestration of Prague' (incident when Bohemians claiming independence throw two Catholic governors from a window) starts Thirty Years War of religion – general conflict in Europe until 1648.

1624 Richelieu becomes First Minister of France – 1642.

1625 Denmark enters Thirty Years War on Protestant side.

1625–1649 Charles I, king of England. Parliamentary opposition continues on number of counts: (i) Charles stating himself to be above the law; (ii) favouring bishops while others want a more Puritan worship; (iii) in desperate need of money for armies, he imposes taxes.

1627–1628 Siege of La Rochelle (Huguenots) by Richelieu. La Rochelle surrenders – end of political power for Huguenots.

1629 Charles I dissolves parliament – personal rule until 1640. Treaty of Lübeck between Ferdinand II, Holy Roman emperor, and Christian IV of Denmark.

1630 King Gustavus Adolphus II of Sweden enters war against Ferdinand II.

1631 Catholics under Tilly sack Magdeburg. Battle of Leipzig – Swedes and Saxons defeat Tilly.

1632 Battle of Lützen – Swedish victory over Catholic forces but Gustavus Adolphus killed.

1634 Battle of Nordlingen – imperial forces defeat Swedes.

1635 Treaty of Prague: Ferdinand II makes peace with Saxony – accepted by most Protestant princes.

1640 Charles I summons Short Parliament – which he dissolves when it fails to grant him money.

1640–1653 Long Parliament in England.

1641 Revolt of Irish Catholics – 30,000 Protestants massacred. Charles I marches to Westminster to arrest 5 members of the Commons. Attempt fails, he flees to Hampton Court.

1642 Outbreaks of Civil War in England between Royalists (Cavaliers) and Parliamentarians (Roundheads). Battle of Edgehill indecisive.

1643–1645 Denmark fights Sweden for Baltic supremacy.

1644 Battle of Marston Moor – Prince Rupert defeated.

1645 Cromwell forms Model Army: Battle of Naseby – Parliamentarians defeat Charles I.

1646 Charles I surrenders to the Scots.

1647 Charles handed over to Parliamentarians. Escapes and makes secret treaty with the Scots.

1648 Scots invade England – defeated at Preston by Cromwell. Treaty of Westphalia: ends Thirty Years War – Dutch and Swiss Republics recognized as independent.

1648–1649 *Fronde* (Parliamentary) rebellion in Paris against Louis XIV.

1649 Execution of Charles I – the Commonwealth (Republic) to 1660.

ELSEWHERE

1602–1618 War between Persia and Turkey.

1603 Tokugawa appointed shogun in Japan.

1604 Foundation of French East India Company.

1605–1627 India: Jahangir, Mughal emperor.

1607 Henry Hudson voyages to Greenland and up Hudson River.

1615 China: Tribes in north form military organization – later called *Manchus*.

1616 Willem Schouten, Dutch navigator, rounds Cape Horn. British East India Company trades with Persia from Surat (seat of British in India).

1619 Representative assembly at Jamestown, Virginia – first in American colonies. First Negro slaves arrive in Virginia.

1620 Puritan Pilgrim Fathers from England reach Cape Cod in *Mayflower* and found New Plymouth (later Boston).

1621 China: Nurhachi expels the Ming and sets up Manchu capital at Loyang.

1624 Virginia becomes a crown colony.

1626 Dutch found New Amsterdam (later New York).

1628–1658 India: Shah Jehan – poor ruler but responsible for Taj Mahal (1632–1653) as tomb for his wife.

1630 Ottoman Turks under Murad IV take Hamadan (Persia).

1638 Turks conquer Baghdad.

1641 Japan: Only Dutch retain a trading post on an island in Nagasaki Harbour. Japan is virtually cut off from world.

1642 French found Montreal.

1644–1912 Manchu (Tu Ch'ing) dynasty in China.

1645–1664 War between Turkey and Venice.

1650 Ali Bey makes himself hereditary bey (governor) of Tunis.

BALANCE OF POWER 1650–1840

At the beginning of this period Europe was still ruled by powerful monarchies and especially France under Louis XIV. After the French Revolution (1789–1793) and the Napoleonic Wars the ideas of democracy and nationalism came to dominate European thinking. It was also a time of great scientific and literary advances.

Gustavus Adolphus of Sweden – 'the Lion of the North'– was an inspiring leader who made Sweden the greatest power in northern Europe.

EUROPE

1652–1654 Anglo-Dutch War.
1660 Restoration of Charles II (Catholic) to throne of England.
1661 Louis XIV absolute monarch in France.
1665 Great Plague of London.
1665–1667 Second Anglo-Dutch War.
1666 Great Fire of London.
1672 William III (of Orange), ruler of the Netherlands.
1685 Louis XIV of France revokes the Edict of Nantes. All religions except Catholicism banned.
1686 League of Augsburg – coalition of European princes against Louis XIV, who was claiming one of the German states.
1688 The 'Glorious Revolution' in England. William III of the Netherlands invited to save England from Catholicism. James II flees to France. William III and his wife Mary II become joint rulers of England and Scotland.
1689–1725 Peter I, tsar of Russia.
1690 William III defeats exiled James II at the Battle of the Boyne in Ireland.
1697 Treaty of Ryswick ends war against France by League of Augsburg.
1700–1721 Great Northern War for supremacy in the Baltic.
1701 Act of Settlement establishes Protestant Hanoverian succession in Britain.
1701–1713 War of Spanish Succession.
1707 Act of Union between England and Scotland – now named Great Britain.
1713 Treaty of Utrecht ends war of Spanish Succession.
1715 First Jacobite uprising in Scotland.
1740–1748 War of Austrian Succession.
1745 Jacobite rebellion (in Scotland).
1756–1763 Seven Years War between Britain and France.
1762–1796 Catherine the Great, tsarina of Russia.
1772 First partition of Poland.
1773 Peasant uprising in Russia.
1783 Treaty of Paris recognizes American independence.

ELSEWHERE

1652 Africa: Capetown founded by the Dutch.
1661 India: English acquire Bombay.
1664 America: English seize New Amsterdam from Dutch and rename it New York – leads to war.
1669 India: Aurangzeb prohibits Hindu religion. Venice surrenders Crete to Turkey.
1670 America: English Hudson Bay Company founded.
1682 America: La Salle takes Mississippi Valley for France.
1692 Salem witchcraft trials in New England.
1699 America: French establish colony of Louisiana.
1707 India: Death of Aurangzeb leads to disintegration of Mughal empire.
1744–1748 America: War between Britain and France – King George's War.
1745 Canada: Britain captures Louisburg.
1751 India: Clive takes Arcot – beginning of British ascendancy.
1759 Canada: British capture Quebec from French.
1763 Peace of Paris ends Seven Years War – Britain gains Canada and most land west of the Mississippi.
America: Chief Pontiac leads Indian uprising.
1767 America: Townshend Acts impose tax on imports.
Mason-Dixon line divides free states from slave states.
1770 America: Boston massacre – British troops fire on mob.
James Cook discovers Australia.
1773 America: Boston Tea Party.
1774 India: Warren Hastings appointed first Governor-General.
1775–1783 American War of Independence.
1776 American Declaration of Independence.
1777 Christianity introduced in Korea.

The British forces surrendered to the Americans at Yorktown, Virginia in October 1781.

TECHNOLOGY

1661 Robert Boyle defines chemical elements.
1665 Isaac Newton experiments with gravitation; invents differential calculus.
1666 First Cheddar cheese.
1667 French army uses hand grenades.
1668 Reflecting telescope invented by Newton.
1680 Dodo, flightless bird, extinct.
1701–1744 Anders Celsius, Swiss astronomer who invents centigrade thermometer (1742).
1705 Edmund Halley correctly predicts the return in 1758 of the comet seen in 1682.
1714 D. G. Fahrenheit constructs mercury thermometer with temperature scale.
1718 Machine gun patented by James Puckle of London.
1733 John Kay patents his flying shuttle loom.
1735 Linnaeus writes his classification of nature.
1752 Benjamin Franklin invents lightning conductor.
1760 Botanical Gardens opened at Kew, London.
1766 Henry Cavendish, English scientist, discovers hydrogen less dense than air.
1767 First successful spinning machine invented by James Hargreaves.
1769 Arkwright's water powered spinning machine.
1774 Joseph Priestley discovers oxygen.
Austrian physician, F. A. Mesmer (1733–1815), uses hypnosis for health purposes.
1775 James Watt, Scottish scientist, perfects his invention of the steam engine.
1780 Scheller constructs first fountain pen.
1783 Montgolfier brothers ascend in hot air balloon at Annonay, France.
1784 George Atwood, English mathematician, accurately determines acceleration of a free-falling body.
Andrew Meikle, Scottish millwright, invents threshing machine.

Benjamin Franklin, the American scientist and statesman, demonstrating the electrical nature of lightning by flying a kite in a thunderstorm and drawing sparks from a key tied to the lower end of its string.

CULTURE

1662 Louis XIV begins to build Palace of Versailles.
1666 Antonio Stradivari labels his first violin.
1608–1674 John Milton, English poet writes 'Paradise Lost' (1667–1674).
1667–1745 Johnathan Swift, English author of *Gulliver's Travels* (1726).
1675 Paris becomes centre of European culture.
1675–1741 Antonio Vivaldi, Italian composer of *The Four Seasons*.
1680 Comédie Française formed.
1684–1721 Jean Antoine Watteau, French painter.
1685–1750 J. S. Bach, German composer.
1685–1759 George Frederick Handel, German composer.
1694–1778 Voltaire, French writer and philosopher.
1698 Tax on beards in Russia.
1700 Unmarried women taxed in Berlin.
1707–1793 Carlo Goldoni, Venetian dramatist.
1709 Invention of the pianoforte by Bartolomeo Cristofori.
1718 Porcelain manufactured for first time in Vienna.
1724–1804 Immanuel Kant, German philosopher.
1731 10 Downing Street, London residence of British Prime Ministers built.
1732 Covent Garden opera house opens.
1732–1799 Beaumarchais, French dramatist.
1732–1806 Jean Honoré Fragonard, French painter.
1746–1828 Francisco de Goya, Spanish painter.
1748–1825 Jacques Louis David, French Classical painter.
1749–1832 Johann Goethe, German Romantic writer.
1755 Samuel Johnson (1709–1784) writes *Dictionary of the English Language*.
1756–1791 Wolfgang Mozart, Austrian composer.
1762 Jean Jacques Rousseau (1712–1778): *Social Contract*.
1770–1827 Ludwig van Beethoven, German composer.
1770–1850 William Wordsworth, English poet.
1775 Jane Austen, English writer.
1775–1851 J. M. W. Turner, English painter.

EUROPE

1789 French Revolution begins.
1791 New constitution in France.
1792 France declared a republic.
1793–1794 Reign of Terror in France under Robespierre.
1795 Directory rules France.
Coalition of Britain, Austria, Russia, Portugal, Naples and Ottoman empire against France.
1799 Bonaparte sets up Consulate in France to replace Directory.
1801 Act of Union between Great Britain and Ireland to form United Kingdom.
1802 Bonaparte created First Consul.
1804 Bonaparte crowns himself Napoleon, emperor of the French.
1805 Battle of Trafalgar.
1806 Napoleon dissolves Holy Roman empire.
1807 Britain abolishes slave trade.
Treaty of Tilsit between Napoleon and Tsar Alexander.
Napoleon at the height of his power in Europe.
1808–1814 Peninsular War – French occupy Spain.
1812 Napoleon's Russian campaign.
1814 Napoleon abdicates and is exiled to Elba.
1815 Napoleon returns. Final defeat of Napoleon at Waterloo.
1830 July Revolution in Paris overthrows Charles X.
1832 Reform Act passed in Britain – extends vote to the middle classes.

The storming of the Bastille, a fortress prison in Paris, on 14 July 1789. This event marked the start of the French Revolution.

ELSEWHERE

1783 America: Britain recognizes independence of the Thirteen Colonies.
India Act gives Britain control of political affairs.
1787 Britain establishes colony of Sierra Leone.
1788 First British convicts transported to Australia.
1789 George Washington, first president of United States (USA).
1791 Canada Act – divides Canada into English and French-speaking territories.
1795 Africa: British take Cape of Good Hope from the Dutch.
1803 America: Louisiana Purchase – France sells Louisiana to USA.
1804 Haiti becomes independent of France.
1810 Argentina independent.
1811 Paraguay and Venezuela independent.
1815 France prohibits slave trade.
1818 Chaka the Great founds Zulu empire in southern Africa.
1819 Bolivar secures the independence of Great Colombia.
Spain cedes Florida to USA.
1820–1822 Egyptians conquer Sudan and found Khartoum.
1821 Peru and Mexico independent.
1822 Brazil independent of Portugal.
1823 Proclamation of the Monroe Doctrine by the president of USA warning Europe not to interfere in American politics.
1825 Bolivia independent.
1830 French invade Algeria.
1833 Abolition of slavery in British empire.
1835–1837 Great Trek by Boers from Cape to found Transvaal.
1836 Texas independent of Mexico after battle of Alamo.
1839–1842 First Opium War between Britain and China.
1839 British occupy Aden.

TECHNOLOGY

1785 Salsano invents seismograph.
Power loom invented by Cartwright.
1790 Lavoisier produces his table of 31 chemical elements.
1793 Eli Whitney invents the cotton gin in USA.
1794 First telegraph – Paris-Lille.
First technical college – École Polytechnique – opens in Paris.
1795 François Appert designs preserving jar for foods.
1796 Edward Jenner, English physician, introduces vaccination against smallpox.
1800 Alessandro Volta produces the first electric battery.
1802 John Dalton, English physicist, introduces atomic theory into chemistry.
1803 Robert Fulton propels a boat by steam power (also inventor of torpedo).
Henry Shrapnel invents shells.
1815 Humphrey Davy, English chemist, invents miner's lamp.
1819 Steamship *Savannah* crosses the Atlantic.
Stethoscope invented by René Laennec.
1822 Shell gun invented by Henri J. Paihans of France.
1825 Opening of Stockton-Darlington railroad – first line to carry passengers.
1829 George Stephenson's engine: 'The Rocket'.
1830–1833 *Principles of Geology* by Sir Charles Lyell.
First railroads in France and U.S.A.
1831 Dynamo and transformer invented by Michael Faraday.
1835 Photography – negative/positive process developed by William Fox Talbot.
1836 Invention of revolver by Samuel Colt.
1840 Introduction of the Penny Post in Britain.

CULTURE

1785 *The Times* newspaper begun by John Walter.
1788–1824 Lord Byron, English poet.
1790–1824 Théodore Géricault, French painter.
1793 The Louvre, Paris, becomes national art gallery.
1795–1821 John Keats, English poet.
1798 Essay on population by Thomas Robert Malthus.
1799 Rosetta stone found near Rosetta, Egypt, makes the deciphering of hieroglyphics possible.
1799–1850 Honoré de Balzac, French writer.
1799–1863 Delacroix, French painter.
1802–1885 Victor Hugo, French writer.
1803–1882 Robert Waldo Emerson, U.S. philosopher.
1804–1849 Johann Strauss, Austrian composer.
1812 Elgin Marbles brought to England.
1813–1883 Richard Wagner, German composer.
1819–1877 Gustave Courbet, French painter.
1821–1880 Gustave Flaubert, French writer.
1828–1910 Leo Tolstoy, Russian writer.

FIRST PHOTOGRAPHY

Fox Talbot's picture of Lacock Abbey, Wiltshire, was made in 1843. He used the Calotype process which he had invented in 1835. It was the first negative/positive process and meant that any number of prints could be made from the one negative. A Frenchman, Joseph Niéphore Niépce is credited with 'the first photograph made by a camera'. There still exists a photograph he made in 1826.

Fox Talbot's 'negative' of a view of Lacock Abbey.

A print made from the same negative.

EUROPE

1650 Second *fronde* rebellion in France – suppressed.
Charles II lands in Scotland and is proclaimed king.
1651 Battle of Worcester – Charles II defeated by Cromwell and flees abroad again.
1652–1654 First Anglo-Dutch War.
1653 Cromwell becomes Lord Protector of England.
1658 Death of Cromwell – succeeded by son Richard.
1660 Charles II restored to throne by parliament in England – reigns to 1685.
Death of Cardinal Mazarin – Louis XIV becomes absolute monarch.
1665 Great Plague in London.
1665–1667 Second Anglo-Dutch War.
1666 Great Fire of London.
1667 Dutch fleet defeats English in river Medway.
1668 Triple Alliance of England, Holland and Sweden against France.
Treaty of Lisbon – Spain recognizes independence of Portugal.
Treaty of Aix-la-Chapelle ends war between France and Spain.
1670 Secret Treaty of Dover between Charles II and Louis XIV to restore Catholicism in England.
1672 William III (Orange) becomes hereditary *Stadholder* (ruler) of Netherlands – to 1702.
1672 Third Anglo-Dutch War.
1672–1678 France at war with Netherlands.
1677 William III of Netherlands marries Mary, daughter of James, Duke of York, Catholic heir to the English throne.
1678 Popish plot in England – Titus Oates falsely accuses Catholics of plan to murder Charles II.
1679 Act of Habeas Corpus passed in England, forbidding imprisonment without trial.
Parliament's Bill of Exclusion against the Duke of York blocked by Charles II – Parliament dismissed. Charles II rejects petitions calling for a new parliament. Petitioners become known as *Whigs*, their opponents (royalists) known as *Tories*.
1680 Louis XIV establishes Chambers of Reunion – France occupies Strasbourg, Luxembourg, Lorraine.
1685 Louis XIV revokes the Edict of Nantes – all religions banned in France except Catholicism.
1685–1688 James II, king of England.
1686 League of Augsburg is formed against France.
1688 The 'Glorious Revolution' in England – William III of Holland is invited to save the country from Catholicism. James flees to France.
1689 Bill of Rights in England – establishes principle of constitutional monarchy and bars Catholics from the throne.
William III and Mary II joint rule to 1694.
1689–1725 Peter I (the Great), tsar of Russia.
1690 Defeat of exiled James II by William III at battle of the Boyne in Ireland.
1692 Battle of La Hogue – Anglo-Dutch fleet defeats French.
1694 Death of Mary II – William III sole ruler of England to 1702.
1695 First penal laws against Catholics in Ireland.
1697 Treaty of Ryswick ends war of League of Augsburg against France.
1700 Charles II of Spain names Philip of Anjou, grandson of Louis XIV as his heir – Philip becomes the V of Spain to 1746.
Battle of Narva – Charles XII of Sweden defeats Russians.

TURKEY & EUROPE

1656 Venetians rout the Turks off the Dardanelles.
1661–1664 Turkey at war with the Holy Roman empire.
1664 Battle of St Gotthard – Austrians defeat Turks.
1669 Venice surrenders Crete to Turkey.
1672–1676 Turkey at war with Poland for control of Ukraine.
1676 Treaty of Zuravno – Turkey gains Polish Ukraine.
1677–1681 Turkey at war with Russia.
1681 Treaty of Radzin – Russia gains most of Turkish Ukraine.
1682–1699 Turkey at war with Austria.
1683 Turks besiege Vienna – city relieved by German and Polish troops.
1684 Pope Innocent XI forms the Holy League of Venice, Austria and Poland against Turkey.
1686 Venice takes Peloponnese from Turks.
1687 Battle of Mohacs – Turks are defeated and the Habsburg succession to the Hungarian throne is confirmed.
1697 Battle of Zenta – Eugène of Savoy defeats Turks.
1699 Treaty of Karlowitz – Austria receives Hungary from Turkey; Venice gains Peloponnese and parts of Yugoslavia; Poland takes Turkish Ukraine.

ELSEWHERE

1657 Japan: Great fire destroys Edo.

1658–1707 India: Aurangzeb, Mughal emperor – clever but ruthless leader and a bigoted Muslim. Imprisons his father and kills his brothers to gain throne.

1660 Africa: Rise of Bambara kingdom on upper Niger River.

1661 India: English acquire Bombay.
Chinese under Koxinga take Formosa (Taiwan).

1662 N. Africa: Portugal cedes Tangier to England.

1666–1688 India: Aurangzeb at war with Muhammadans in central India and with peoples of north-east India.

1669 India: Aurangzeb prohibits the Hindu religion and persecutes Hindus.

1676–1678 India: Sikh uprisings against Aurangzeb.

1680–1709 Tsunayohi, shogun of Japan.

1683 China: Koxinga's grandson surrenders Formosa to the Manchus.

1684 N. Africa: English abandon Tangier to sultan of Morocco.
French expeditions against Algerian pirates.

1685 India: Aurangzeb seizes Surat – expels English.

1686 Africa: Louis XIV proclaims French annexation of Madagascar.
America: Dominion of New England formed.

1688–1704 Japan: Rise of merchant class.

1690 India: English allowed to return to Bengal at Calcutta by Aurangzeb.

1691 China: Emperor reorganizes Mongolia.

1697 Africa: French complete their conquest of the Dutch in Senegal.

1699 USA: French establish colony of Louisiana.

HIGH FASHION

Left: A Puritan dressed in sombre clothes and a Cavalier in more flamboyant dress.

A coach of the 17th century.

Characters from Molière's *Comédie Française*.

A French gentleman in a felt hat and campaign wig in which are tied ribbons known as 'favours' – love tokens from the woman he has left behind to go to war.

LOUIS XIV

Louis XIV, the 'Sun King', came to the throne of France as a boy of five in 1643. He assumed full powers in 1661 on the death of his chief minister, Cardinal Mazarin. He ruled as an 'absolute' monarch – he once said 'L'état, c'est moi' (I am the state) – until his death in 1715. Under him France was the most powerful country in Europe. Louis' court was the most splendid in Europe and the palace at Versailles the wonder of the age. But France was almost always at war with her neighbours who feared her ambitions. By centralizing all power in the hands of the monarch Louis sowed the seeds of the French Revolution of 1789.

A painting of Isaac Newton.

Sir Isaac Newton (1642–1727) was a genius whose ideas were part of a great scientific awakening that changed the thinking of his age. He made three momentous discoveries before the age of 26 – the theory of gravitation; that white light is composed of rays of coloured light; and he invented the new mathematical science of calculus. The principles he stated became the basis of modern physics.

EUROPE

1701 Act of Settlement establishes Protestant Hanoverian succession.
1701–1713 War of Spanish Succession following failure of Charles II of Spain to produce an heir.
Grand Alliance of England, Netherlands, Holy Roman empire and German states against France.
Charles XII of Sweden invades Poland.
1703–1711 Hungarian revolt against Austria.
1704 British fleet captures Gibraltar from Spain.
Battle of Blenheim – Duke of Marlborough and Prince Eugène of Savoy (commanding Austrian army) defeat French to save Vienna.
1706 Battle of Ramillies – Marlborough defeats French.
Battle of Turin – Eugène defeats French.
Treaty of Altranstadt between Augustus II of Poland and Charles XII of Sweden.
1707 Act of Union unites England and Scotland.
1708 Battle of Oudenarde – Marlborough and Eugène defeat French.
1709 Battle of Malplaquet – Alliance defeats French but at heavy cost of 20,000 men.
Battle of Poltava – Peter the Great of Russia defeats Charles XII of Sweden. Begins building new capital – St Petersburg.
1713 Treaty of Utrecht ends War of Spanish Succession – France cedes Newfoundland, Nova Scotia and Hudson Bay to Britain and recognizes the Protestant Succession.
1714–1727 George I, first Hanoverian, king of Great Britain.
1715 Jacobite rising in Scotland for James Edward, the Old Pretender, son of James II.
1720 Collapse of John Law's Mississippi Company in France.
South Sea Bubble in England – financial panic.
1721–1742 Sir Robert Walpole, the first British prime minister.
1725 Treaty of Vienna between Austria (Savoy) and Spain.
Catherine, widow of Peter I, becomes Catherine I of Russia.
1727–1729 Spain at war with Britain and France.
1733 Family pact between Bourbons of France and Spain.
1733–1735 War of Polish Succession after death of Augustus.
1738 Treaty of Vienna settles War of Polish Succession.
1739–1741 War of Jenkin's Ear between Britain and Spain.
1740–1786 Frederick II (the Great), king of Prussia – seizes Silesia (1740), an Austrian province sparking off War of Austrian Succession.
1740–1748 War of Austrian Succession caused by death of last male descendant of Habsburg family, Charles VI and failure by rivals, Bavaria, Spain and Saxony (supported by Poland and France) to recognize Maria-Theresa as empress, (supported by Hungary, Britain and Netherlands).
1743 Battle of Dettingen – French defeated by Hanoverians and Britain.
1744 Frederick the Great (Prussia) invades Bohemia but is defeated by Austrian and Saxon forces.
1745 'Forty Five' rebellion by Charles Edward Stuart, the Young Pretender, in Scotland.
Alliance by Austria, Britain, Netherlands and Saxony against Prussia.
Bavaria is defeated and withdraws claim to Austrian throne.
Battle of Fontenoy – French defeat British.
Francis I, husband of Maria Theresa, is elected Holy Roman emperor (to 1765) securing Maria Theresa's postion in Europe.
1746 Battle of Culloden – Jacobites are defeated in Britain.
1748 Treaty of Aix-la-Chapelle ends the War of Austrian Succession.

MIDDLE ASIA

1707 Death of Aurangzeb is followed by disintegration of Mughal empire.
1709–1711 Afghans rise against Persians – establish Afghan state.
1710–1711 Turkey and Russia at war – Peter the Great buys peace.
1715 English East India Company gains tax and other exemptions in India.
1718 Treaty of Passarowitz ends war between Turkey and Austria.
1724 Russo-Turkish agreement to dismember Persia.
Hyderabad (central India) achieves independence from the Mughal empire.
1726 Persia defeats Turks.
1730–1735 Maratha government gains ascendancy in India.
1735 Russians give up their Persian conquests and unite with Persians against Turkey.
1736–1739 Turkey at war with Russia and Austria.
1738 Nadir Shah, ruler of Persia (1736–1747), invades northern India – captures Kandahar.
1739 Nadir Shah sacks Delhi to reach height of his power.
Treaty of Belgrade ends war between Turkey, Austria and Russia – Austria gives up Serbia and Belgrade to Turkey.
1746 French capture Madras from English.
1747 Nadir Shah is assassinated and a period of anarchy follows in Persia to 1750.
1748 English regain Madras – the beginning of Anglo-French rivalry in India.

SPORT AND INVENTION

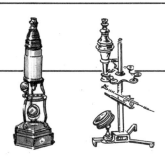

Microscopes of the mid-18th century.

Newcomen's steam engine of 1647.

Windmill with a fantail. The fantail, invented in 1745, turns the sails into the wind whenever the wind direction changes.

Hunters on horseback shooting pheasant.

The drill plough of 1745 dropped the seed immediately the ground had been ploughed.

Otters were hunted almost to extinction during the 18th century.

THE SLAVE TRADE

Sugar plantations in the new European colonies of the West Indies and cotton plantations in the southern states of North America required cheap labour. This caused the growth of the Atlantic slave trade which lasted for three centuries. Britain earned enormous wealth supplying slaves from West Africa to the Americas. In the 18th century between nine to ten million Africans were shipped across the Atlantic on the dreaded 'middle passage'. Many died on the way. Slavery was abolished throughout the British Empire in 1833.

ELSEWHERE

1705 Africa: Hussein Ibn Ali founds the Husseinite dynasty in Tunis and throws off Turkish control.
1709–1745 Japan: Period of reform.
1712 China: Period of prosperity in China.
1713 S. America: Britain gains the *asiento* (contract) to supply slaves to Spanish America from west Africa – the most active period of British slave trade.
1714 Africa: Ahmed Bey makes himself bey (governor) of Tripoli – founds Karamanli dynasty.
1720 China: Imperial garrisons established in Tibet.
Japan: Ban removed on the study of Europe and European books but not religion.
1721 China: Revolt in Formosa. Edo (Tokyo) has population of 800,000, largest city in the world.
1723 Africa: Bartholomew Stibbs takes possession of Gambia region for the British Africa Company.
1723–1735 China: Peace at home but war against the Mongols.
1727 China: Kiakhta Treaty fixes borders between China and Russia.
1732–1733 Japan: Great famine in western Japan.
1733 USA: Foundation of Georgia, the last of the Thirteen Colonies in North America.
1736–1795 China: Imperial control is extended throughout central Asia – a period of wealth.
1742 Japan: Codification of criminal law.
1744–1748 USA: War between Britain and France – King George's War.
1745 Canada: British capture Louisburg, French fortress.

67

EUROPE

1756 Treaty of Westminster – alliance of Britain and Prussia.
Treaty of Versailles – alliance of France and Austria.
Beginning of the Seven Years' War – result of Anglo-French rivalry in the colonies and Austro-Prussian antagonism in Europe.
1757 Russia joins the French alliance.
1758 Battle of Zorndorf – Prussians defeat Russians.
1759 Battle of Quiberon Bay – British fleet defeats the French.
1762 Britain declares war on Spain.
Treaty of St Petersburg between Russia and Prussia.
1763 Peace of Paris between Britain, France and Spain ends Seven Years' War.
Peace of Hubertsburg between Prussia, Saxony and Austria.
1772 First partition of Poland among Austria, Prussia and Russia.
1773–1775 Cossack Pugachev leads peasant uprising in Russia.
1775 Beginning of American War of Independence.
1778 France joins American War against Britain.
1779–1783 France and Spain besiege Gibraltar but fail to capture.
1780 Armed Neutrality of the North: Russia, Denmark, Sweden, Netherlands join to protect neutral shipping from British interference.
1783 Treaty of Paris ends American War of Independence.
Russia annexes Crimea.
1787 Assembly of Notables dismissed in France after refusing to introduce financial reforms.
1789 Estates-General called in France.
Storming of the Bastille – beginning of French Revolution.
Third Estate forms a National Assembly which governs France as a Constituent Assembly until 1791.
1792 France at war against Austria and Prussia.
1792–1795 National Convention governs France which declares itself a republic on September 21, 1792.
1793 Louis XVI and his wife, Marie Antoinette, executed.
Revolutionary France declares war on Britain, the Netherlands and Spain.
1793–1794 Reign of Terror in France – Robespierre and Committee of Public Safety rule the country.
1794 French invade Dutch Republic; occupy Netherlands.
Execution of Danton and Robespierre – ends Reign of Terror.
1795 Treaty of Basle between France and Prussia; Spain makes peace with France; the 5-man Directory rules France.
Partition of the remainder of Poland between Austria, Prussia and Russia.
1796–1797 The Corsican, Napoleon Bonaparte, leads French army to conquer most of Italy.
1797 British naval mutinies at Spithead and Nore.
Battle of Cape St Vincent – British defeat Franco-Spanish fleet.
1798 Rebellion in Ireland (Battle of Vinegar Hill).
French occupy Rome and establish Roman republic.
French invade Switzerland and set up Helvetic republic.
1799 Coalition of powers (Britain, Austria, Russia, Portugal, Naples and Turkey) against France; battles of Zürich, Trebbia and Novi – French driven from Italy.
Bonaparte returns to France, overthrows Directory and sets up Consulate which he heads to 1804.
1800 French defeat Austrians at the battles of Marengo and Hohenlinden.

ASIA

1751 India: Robert Clive takes Arcot – ends French plans for supremacy in south.
1756 India: Black Hole of Calcutta – Suruj-ud-Daulah, nawab of Bengal, imprisons 146 British in small room, most die.
1757 India: Clive captures Calcutta.
Battle of Plassey – Clive defeats the nawab of Bengal. Start of British ascendancy.
1757–1843 China restricts foreign trade to Canton.
1761 India: Battle of Panipat – Afghans defeat Marathas.
1774 Turkey: Treaty of Kuchuk Kainarji – Russia gains Black Sea ports and the right to represent Greek Orthodox Church in Turkey.
India: Regulating Act – British India to be ruled by a Governor-General and Council. Warren Hastings appointed first Governor-General.
1775–1782 India: British at war with Marathas.
1782 India: Treaty of Salbai ends British-Maratha war.
1784 India Act: British government in Westminster to control political affairs.
1786–1787 Indonesia: Chinese suppress a revolt in Formosa.
1787 Japan: Rice riots at Edo, following great famine.
1794–1925 Persia: Aga Muhammad founds the Qaja dynasty.
1796 British take Ceylon from Dutch.
1799 India: Tippoo Sahib, ruler of Mysore killed in battle fighting British – British control is established over southern India.

ELSEWHERE

1759 British capture Quebec.
1767 USA: Mason-Dixon line separates the free and slave states.
1770 USA: Boston Massacre – British troops fire on Boston mob and kill five citizens. Repeal of the Townshend Tax Acts but a tax is retained by Britain on imported tea.
1773 Boston Tea Party – citizens, disguised as Indians, dump tea in Boston harbour.
1775 American War of Independence to 1783. Battles of Lexington and Concord – Americans led by George Washington.
1776 USA: British troops evacuate Boston. American Declaration of Independence.
1777 USA: Battle of Saratoga – the British surrender.
1778 USA: France joins the war on the side of the colonists.
1780–1783 S. America: Peruvian Indians under Inca, Tupac Amara, revolt against Spain.
1781 USA: Surrender of British troops at Yorktown.
1783 USA: Treaty of Paris – end of American War of Independence. Britain recognizes independence of the 13 colonies.
1787 USA: New constitution is drawn up.
1789–1797 George Washington, first American president.
1791 Canada Act – divides Canada into English and French-speaking territories. USA: Bill of Rights – the first 10 Amendments to US Constitution.
1798–1799 Africa: Bonaparte's expedition to Egypt – battle of the Pyramids; Cairo taken by the French. Battle of the Nile – Nelson defeats the French fleet.
1799 Napoleon invades Syria.

AIR, LAND AND WATER

A hot air balloon over Versailles in 1783. By the middle of the 19th century balloons were widely used in battle to spot enemy troop movement.

Royal mail coach in 1820. The fastest vehicle on the road, it travelled at 16km/h and could carry nine passengers.

Karl von Drais' dandyhorse of 1817. It had no pedals.

A Mississippi sternwheeler steam boat of 1820.

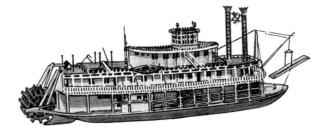

THE FRENCH REVOLUTION

The French Revolution began on 14 July, 1789, with the storming of the Bastille. Faced with state bankruptcy, Louis XVI called the Estates-General, a national parliament which had not met since 1614. When the commons found they were always outvoted by the nobility and clergy they formed a Constituent Assembly pledged to create a new constitution. In 1791, after the king tried to flee, the mob stormed the royal palace of the Tuileries. The National Convention (assembly) abolished the monarchy and established a republic. The king was executed. The impact of the revolution whose three catchwords were Liberty, Equality, Fraternity influenced European politics throughout the 19th century.

EUROPE

1804 Bonaparte crowns himself Napoleon I.

1804–1813 Serbs revolt against Turks.

1805 Battle of Trafalgar – British fleet under Nelson defeats Franco-Spanish fleet.

Battle of Austerlitz – French defeat Austro-Russian forces.

1806 Napoleon dissolves the Holy Roman empire and replaces it with the Confederation of the Rhine.

1808 French occupy Spain.

Peninsular War in Spain to 1814 – British troops with Spanish and Portuguese oppose the French.

1809 Battle of Corunna – French defeat British.

1811 Luddite riots in England against mechanization of textile industry.

George III declared insane, Prince of Wales becomes Regent.

1812 Napoleon invades Russia with the Grand Army – the battle of Borodino – French occupy Moscow, but then have to retreat.

1813 Battle of Vittoria – French driven from Spain by Wellington.

1814 Napoleon abdicates and is exiled to Elba.

1814–1815 Congress of Vienna – heads of state discuss settlement of post-war Europe.

1815 The Hundred Days – Napoleon escapes from Elba and marches on Paris.

Battle of Waterloo – Napoleon defeated by British under Wellington and exiled to St Helena.

Quadruple Alliance of Britain, Austria, Prussia and Russia to maintain the Congress system.

1818 Congress of Aix-la-Chapelle allows France to join the great powers, to form the Quintuple Alliance.

1819 Peterloo Massacre in England – cavalry charge political meeting in England, several killed.

1820 Liberal revolutions in Spain, Portugal and Italy.

1821–1829 Greek War of Independence from Turkey.

1824 Decembrist uprising against the Tsar Nicholas.

1829 Catholic Emancipation Act in Britain.

1830 July Revolution overthrows Charles X of France.

Revolution against Dutch rule in Belgium.

1832 Reform Act in Britain extends vote to middle classes.

1833 Factory Act in Britain – children under nine may not be employed.

Slavery abolished throughout British empire.

1834 Tolpuddle Martyrs – 6 Dorset labourers transported for trying to form a trade union.

1834–1839 Carlist Wars in Spain – the Pretender, Don Carlos, attempts to gain Spanish throne.

1836 Beginning of Chartist Movement in Britain which demands votes for all adult males.

EUROPE & AFRICA

1803 Australia: Flinders circumnavigates.

USA: Louisiana Purchase – France sells Louisiana Territory for $15m.

1804–1805 American explorers Meriwether Lewis and William Clark explore north-west USA and reach the Pacific.

1805 Egypt: Selim III, sultan of Turkey, appoints Muhammad Ali as pasha of Egypt.

China: Christian literature is banned.

1811 Egypt: Ruling Mamelukes are massacred in Cairo by Muhammad Ali.

1818 Africa: Chaka the Great founds Zulu empire in south.

USA: 49th parallel is fixed as the boundary between USA and Canada.

1819 India: Sikh leader, Ranjit Singh, conquers Kashmir.

Far East: Sir Stamford Raffles founds the British colony of Singapore.

1820 Africa: 4000 British settlers at Albany (Durban) on east coast of South Africa.

1822 Africa: Liberia in west is founded as a colony for freed US slaves.

1823 US President James Monroe issues Monroe Doctrine warning European powers not to intervene in the Americas.

1824–1826 Burma: First Anglo-Burmese war – Britain begins annexation.

1824–1827 Africa: First Ashanti War between Britain and the Ashanti of the Gold Coast (Ghana).

1829 S. America: Greater Colombia is divided into Colombia, Venezuela, Ecuador, New Granada.

1830 Africa: French invade Algeria and depose the ruler *(bey)*.

1833–1835 Voyage of Captain Fitzroy and Charles Darwin in the *Beagle* to Tahiti and New Zealand (scientific).

1835–1837 Africa: Great Trek of Boers in South Africa inland from the Cape – the foundation of Transvaal.

1838 Battle of Blood River – Boers in Natal defeat the Zulus.

1839 British occupy Aden.

1839–1842 First Opium War between Britain and China after Chinese commissioner Lin destroys opium shipments. War puts pressure on weak Manchus to open its doors to European trade.

1840 Treaty of Waitangi – New Zealand becomes a British Crown Colony.

THE MODERN WORLD 1840–1988

Two world wars, nuclear weapons, voyages in space have altered our world beyond recognition since the beginning of this modern age (1840) when postage stamps were first introduced. The greatest problems we now face come from a world population that has passed the five thousand million mark and is putting huge strains upon all our resources.

A blaze of lights – New York City by night.

EUROPE & AFRICA

1846 Zulu reserves set up in Natal, South Africa.
1848 Year of revolutions in Europe.
1853–1856 David Livingstone crosses Africa.
1866 Austro-Prussian War over Schleswig – Holstein. Austria defeated.
1869 Suez Canal opened.
1870–1871 Franco-Prussian War because of French resentment at growing power of Prussia – defeat of France and emergence of united Germany.
1871 Unification of Italy.
1877 Russia at war with Turkey over the Balkans. Transvaal (South Africa) annexed by Britain.
1897 Britain and France assume control of Egyptian affairs.
Zulu War.
1881 Boers defeat British at Majuba Hill and make Transvaal independent.
1882 Britain occupies Egypt.
1882–1914 Triple Alliance of Germany, Italy and Austria-Hungary.
1884 Berlin Conference signals the 'Scramble for Africa'.
1885 German East Africa established.
1890 Rhodesia founded by Cecil Rhodes.
1893 Ivory Coast becomes a French protectorate.
1896 Ethiopians defeat the Italians at Adowa.
1897 Greece and Turkey at war over Crete.
1898 Battle of Omdurman. British defeat Sudan nationalists.
1899–1902 Anglo-Boer War.
1900 Britain conquers Nigeria.
1904 *Entente cordiale* between Britain and France.
1909 Act of Union of South Africa.
1911 Italy invades Libya.
1914–1918 First World War.
1916 Easter Rising in Ireland.
1917 October revolution in Russia.

Lenin led the Bolsheviks to power in the October Revolution in 1917 in Russia.

ELSEWHERE

1848 Treaty of Guadeloupe Hidalgo gives California and New Mexico to the USA.
1854 Commodore Perry forces Japan to conclude commercial treaty with the USA.
1856–1860 Anglo-Chinese War.
1857 Indian Mutiny.
1858 India Bill transfers government of India to British Crown.
1860 Anglo-French forces occupy Peking.
1861–1865 American Civil War.
1865 President Lincoln assassinated.
1867 USA buys Alaska from Russia.
1876 Battle of Little Big Horn.
1895 Treaty of Shimonoseki between China and Japan – Japan gains Formosa, Korea independent of China.
1898 American-Spanish War – Cuba becomes independent.
1900 Boxer (Nationalist) rebellion in China.
1904–1905 War between Japan and Russia.
1911 Revolution in Mexico.
1917 USA enters World War I.

General Ulysses S. Grant, the victorious commander of the Union (northern) forces in the US Civil War. In 1868 he was elected the 18th President of the USA.

TECHNOLOGY

1844 Anaesthetic used by US dentist Horace Wells. Morse transmits the first telegraph message.
1853 Hypodermic syringe invented by C. G. Pravaz (France).
1856 Method of mass-producing steel announced by H. Bessemer (GB).
1858 Domestic sewing machine designed by Isaac Singer (US).
1860 Invention of Winchester repeating rifle (US).
1862 Machine gun used in American Civil War, invented by R. J. Gatling.
1866 Dynamite invented by Alfred Nobel (Swed) – he founded the Nobel prizes from the fortune he made from his invention.
1867 Typewriter invented by Christopher Sholes (US).
1874 Riveted Jeans made in San Francisco by J. Davis and Levi Strauss for miners and cowboys.
1876 Telephone invented by Alexander Graham Bell (Scot).
1877 Record player invented by Thomas Edison (US).
Fingerprinting used by W. Hirschel of the Indian civil service to stop army pensioners drawing their pensions twice.
1897 Thomas Edison burned the first successful incandescent filament light bulb for $13\frac{1}{2}$ hours.
1881 Louis Pasteur (Fr) applies immunization to rabies.
1885 First successful petrol-driven car test driven by its inventor Karl Benz (Germany) – on sale in 1888.
First successful submarines are built.
1886 Coca Cola invented by Dr J. Pemberton (US). Launched as 'Esteemed Brain Tonic and Intellectual Beverage'!
1887 Contact lenses invented by Dr Frick (Swiss).
1892 Zip fastener invented by W. L. Judson (US).
1893 First modern breakfast cereal – shredded wheat – invented by H. D. Perky (US).
1895 Sigmund Freud (Aust) publishes first work on psycho-analysis.
Wireless invented by G. Marconi (It.).
Motion pictures presented publicly on screen for the first time by A. L. Lumière in Paris.
William Roetgen (Ger) discovers X-rays.
1901 Safety razor-blades by King Camp Gillette (US).
1903 First aeroplane flight by Wilbur and Orville Wright (US).
1911 Ernest Rutherford (GB) discovers the proton.
1914 Tank invented by Ernest Swinton (GB).
1915 Einstein (Swiss) offers his Theory of Relativity.

CULTURE

1848 Holman Hunt, Millais and D. G. Rossetti found the Pre-Raphaelite Brotherhood in England.
1872 C. Monet (1840–1926; Fr) paints *Impression: Sunrise.*
1874 First Impressionist exhibition in Paris.
1880 *The Thinker* by August Rodin (1840–1914; Fr).
1881 Henry James (1843–1916; USA) writes *Portrait of a Lady.*
1883 R. L. Stevenson (1850–1894; GB) writes *Treasure Island.*
1886 Vincent Van Gogh (1853–1890; Dutch) moves to Paris and meets the French Impressionist painters.
1889 Émile Zola (1840–1902; Fr) writes *Germinal.*
1891 Thomas Hardy (1840–1928; GB) writes *Tess of the d'Urbervilles.*
1893 Anton Dvòrak (1841–1904; Russ) composes *The New World Symphony.*
1895 *Swan Lake* ballet by Tchaikovsky (1840–1893; Russ).
1899 Edward Elgar (1857–1934; GB) composes *Enigma Variations.*
1900 Giacomo Puccini (1858–1924; It) composes *Tosca.*
1901 W. B. Yeats (1865–1939; Irish) assumes leadership of Irish literary revival.
1902 Rudyard Kipling (1865–1936; GB) writes *Just So Stories.*
1904 Anton Chekhov (1860–1964; Russ) writes *The Cherry Orchard.*
1909 Sergei Diaghilev (1872–1929; Russ) forms the *Ballet Russe* in which Nijinsky appears.
1911 Richard Strauss (1864–1949; Austr) composes the opera, *Der Rosenkavalier.*
1912 George Bernard Shaw (1856–1950; GB) writes *Pygmalion.*
1913 Marcel Proust (1871–1922; Fr) starts writing *Remembrance of Things Past.*
Igor Stravinsky (1882–1971; Russ) composes *The Rite of Spring.*

Flyer 1, built by the Wright brothers, was the first machine-powered, heavier-than-air machine to fly (in 1903).

EUROPE & AFRICA

1919 League of Nations formed.
1922 Egypt independent of Britain and France.
Mussolini becomes prime minister of Italy, which becomes a Fascist state (1923).
1926 General strike in Britain.
1933 Hitler becomes chancellor of Germany.
1935 Italians invade Ethiopia.
1936–1939 Spanish Civil War brings Franco to power.
1939–1945 Second World War.
1945 Formation of United Nations.
1949 South African government adopts policy of *apartheid.*
Formation of NATO.
1952 Mau Mau rebellion in Kenya.
1955 Formation of Warsaw Pact in opposition to NATO.
1956 Dispute over Suez Canal.
1957 Treaty of Rome starts the European Community (EC).
1960 17 African colonies become independent.
1961 Berlin Wall built.
1965 Rhodesian government declares independence.
1967 Six Day War between Arabs and Israel.
1967–1970 Nigerian civil war.
1968 Soviet troops invade Czechoslovakia.
1975 October War between Arabs and Israel.
Independence for Portuguese colonies follows the 1974 coup in Portugal.
1979 Downfall of Amin in Uganda.
1980 Rhodesia becomes independent as Zimbabwe.
1981 President Sadat of Egypt assassinated.
Martial Law declared in Poland.
1982 Falklands War – Britain reoccupies islands after Argentine invasion.

Adolf Hitler, the German dictator, at a mass rally of his Nazi party.

AMERICA & ASIA

1920 Prohibition of alcohol in USA.
1924 Sun Yat-sen establishes Chinese Republican government.
1927 Civil war in China.
Charles Lindbergh makes first solo flight across Atlantic.
1929 Collapse of American stock market triggers off world-wide depression.
1931 Japanese occupy Manchuria.
1932 Ottawa Conference – Britain gives trading preferences to Commonwealth.
1934 Mao Zedong leads Communists on Long March.
1937 Japanese invade China.
1941 Japan attacks American fleet at Pearl Harbor, Hawaii.
USA declares war on Axis powers.
1945 First atomic bombs are dropped on Japan.
1946 Civil war in Indo-China.
1947 Marshall Plan for economic recovery in Europe.
India becomes independent – splits into India and Pakistan.
Indonesia becomes independent.
1948 State of Israel is formed.
1949 Communists control all China.
1950 American Senator McCarthy begins inquiry into 'un-American activities'.
1950–1953 Korean War.
1954 French defeated at Dien Bien Phu – Vietnam.
1957 Race riots in southern USA.
1959 Castro comes to power in Cuba.
1960 J. F. Kennedy becomes US President.
1962 Cuban missile crisis.
1964 Civil Rights Bill in USA.
1965 USA sends troops to Vietnam.
1966 'Cultural Revolution' in China.
1968 Martin Luther King and Robert Kennedy assassinated.
1969 American astronauts land on moon.
1971 East Pakistan becomes independent as Bangladesh.
1973 Military overthrow communist Allende in Chile.
USA withdraws from Vietnam.
1974 Watergate scandal forces President Nixon to resign.
1976 Death of Mao Zedong.
1979 Collapse of Shah's regime in Iran – Ayatollah Khomeini sets up an Islamic state.
1980 War between Iran and Iraq.
1982 Israel invades Lebanon.

TECHNOLOGY

1920 Tea bags produced by J. Krieger of San Francisco.
1925 Television invented by John Logie Baird (Scot).
Frozen food process developed by C. Birdseye (US).
1928 Alexander Fleming (GB) discovers penicillin.
First robot built by Captain Richards and A. H. Refell (GB).
1930 Jet engine invented by Frank Whittle (GB).
Planet Pluto is located.
1936 Helicopter designed by Professor Focke (Ger).
1939 First jet aircraft – Heinkel 178 – designed by Dr Okain. First jet fighter – Messerschmitt Me262 – flew in July 1942.
1943 Ball-point pen patented by Hungarian journalist L. Biro.
1944 Automatic digital computer designed by H. Aiken (US).
1948 Transistors devised by Drs Bardeen, Brattain and Shockley (US).
1953 Watson, Crick and Wilkins (GB) discover DNA.
1954 First nuclear submarine USS *Nautilus* launched.
1955 Hovercraft principal patented by C. Cockerell (GB).
Oral contraceptive developed by Dr G. Pincus (US).
1961 Yuri Gagarin (USSR) – first man in space.
Silicon chip integrated circuit patented by Texas Instruments.
1967 Dr Christiaan Barnard (SA) performs heart transplant.
1978 First test-tube baby born following fertilization in a laboratory conducted by Dr Steptoe and Dr Edwards (GB).
1981 First re-usable space shuttle *Columbia* flies.
1987 Astronomers observe a supernova in the Magellanic clouds.

The space rocket Apollo 2 at take-off.

CULTURE

1922 *Ulysses* by James Joyce (1882–1941; Irish). First commercial talking film *Der Brandstift* made in Berlin.
The Waste Land by T. S. Eliot (1885–1965; GB).
1923 George Gershwin (1898–1937; USA), the jazz composer, writes *Rhapsody in Blue*.
Franz Kafka (1883–1924; Ger) writes *The Trial*.
Virginia Woolf (1882–1941; GB) writes *To The Lighthouse*.
1929 Salvador Dali (1904–; Sp) joins Surrealist group of painters.
Ernest Hemingway (1899–1961; USA) writes *A Farewell to Arms*.
1936 Aldous Huxley (1894–1963; GB) writes *Eyeless in Gaza*.
1937 Pablo Picasso (1881–1974; Sp) exhibits his mural *Guernica* which conveys horrors of Spanish Civil War.
1939 Clark Gable and Vivian Leigh star in *Gone with the Wind*.
1941 Henry Moore (1898–1986; GB) produces a series of drawings of refugees in a London air raid shelter.
1945 Benjamin Britten (1913–1976; GB) writes *Peter Grimes*.
1948 Bertold Brecht (1898–1956; Ger) writes *The Caucasian Chalk Circle*.
1949 George Orwell (1903–1950; GB) writes *1984*.
1952 Samuel Beckett (1906–; Irish) writes *Waiting for Godot*.
1959 Gunter Grass (1927–; Ger) writes *The Tin Drum*.
1963 Andy Warhol (1930–1987; USA) and others feature in a show of Pop Art in New York.
1982 Gabriel Garcia Marquez, author of *One Hundred Years of Solitude*, wins Nobel prize.

Superman used in anti-smoking propaganda

EUROPE

1846 Potato famine in Ireland.
Repeal of Corn Laws in Britain.
1848 Year of Revolutions in Europe:
Revolution in Paris – Louis Philippe abdicates and the Second Republic is set up with Louis Napoleon as president.
Revolutions in Milan, Naples, Venice and Rome which are mainly suppressed within the year.
Revolutions in Berlin, Vienna, Prague, Budapest have initial success.
Prince Metternich resigns in Austria and Emperor Ferdinand abdicates.
1849 Revolutions in Italy and Hungary crushed.
1850 Don Pacifico incident – British foreign secretary, Lord Palmerston, defends rights of British citizens abroad.
1852 Louis Napoleon establishes the Second Empire in France as Napoleon III, emperor of France.
1854–1856 Crimean War – Britain, France and Turkey against Russia.
1854 Russians defeated at battles of Balaclava and Inkerman.
Liberal revolution in Spain overthrows government.
1855 Florence Nightingale reforms British army nursing.
1858 Secret alliance between Napoleon III and Count Cavour, prime minister of Piedmont in Italy, determined to liberate Italy from Austrian control.
Irish emigrants in the USA found the Fenian Society.
1859 France and Piedmont at war against Austria: battles of Magenta and Solferino – Austria defeated.
Treaty of Zurich between France and Austria – Piedmont gains Lombardy.
1860 Parma, Modena, Tuscany and Romagna unite with Piedmont.
Italian patriot, Giuseppe Garibaldi and the 1000 Redshirts conquer Sicily and Naples, allying all southern Italy with Piedmont.
1861 Italy, except for Venice and Rome, is united to become a kingdom under Victor Emmanuel, king of Piedmont.
Serfs freed in Russia.
Death of Prince Albert, husband to Queen Victoria.
1863–1864 Polish insurrection fails.
1864 Austria and Prussia take Schleswig-Holstein from Denmark.
1866 Prussia forms alliance with Italy.
Austro-Prussian war over Schleswig-Holstein.
Battle of Sadowa – Prussian victory.
Battles of Custozza and Lissa – Italy defeated by Austrians, but gain Venice.
Treaty of Prague ends Austro-Prussian war after 7 weeks – Austria has to withdraw from German affairs.
1867 Second Reform act in Britain widens the franchise (right to vote).
North German confederation is formed under Prussian leadership.
Formation of Austro-Hungarian monarchy – Franz Joseph of Austria becomes monarch of Hungary.
1869 Disestablishment Act passed in Britain – Irish Church ceases to exist in 1871.
1870 Irish Land Acts – compensation for eviction but this fails to ease the Irish problem.
Kingdom of Italy annexes papal states and Rome becomes the capital of Italy.
1870–1871 Franco-Prussian War.
Battle of Sedan – French defeated, Napoleon III captured, Prussians besiege Paris, end of Second French Empire.

AFRICA & AMERICA

1842 Webster-Ashburton Treaty – settles boundary between the USA and Canada.
1843 Natal becomes a British colony.
1845 Texas joins the USA.
1846 Zulu reserves set up in Natal.
1846–1847 Bantu-British war in South Africa – defeat of Bantus.
1846–1848 War between the USA and Mexico.
1848 California gold rush.
First convention of Women's Rights in New York.
1852 Sand River Convention – Britain recognizes an independent Transvaal.
1853 Livingstone begins crossing Africa.
1860 South Carolina withdraws from the Union (USA).
1861 Abraham Lincoln, president of the USA.
Confederate states of America formed by South Carolina and ten other southern states.
1861–1865 Civil War in USA between Confederates and the Union (north).
1861 Confederates win the battle of Bull Run.
1863 Lincoln proclaims abolition of slavery in USA.
Battle of Gettysburg – Confederate defeat.
French occupy Mexico City.
1864 Union army wins control of Georgia.
1865 End of American Civil War.
President Lincoln assassinated.
1867 Dominion of Canada is established.
France forced to withdraw from Mexico.
1868–1878 Ten Years War – Cuba attempts to win independence from Spain but fails.
1869 Opening of Suez Canal.

ELSEWHERE

1842 Afghanistan: British withdraw from Kabul.

1845–1848 India: British annexation of the Punjab.

1850 Australian Colonies Act – can set up their own legislatures.

1850–1864 China: T'ai Ping rebellion – revolt against the Manchu dynasty.

1852–1853 Second Anglo-Burmese War – British victory, take Pegu.

1854 Japan: Commodore Perry of the US Navy forces Japan to make first commercial treaty with the USA – the Treaty of Kahagawa.

1856 Afghanistan: Persia captures Herat – leads to war with Britain.
Anglo-Chinese War.

1857 Persia: Treaty of Paris ends Anglo-Persian war.
Indian Mutiny – Sepoys (native soldiers) rebel in Bengal army. They take Cawnpore and besiege Lucknow.

1858 India: Relief of Lucknow – end of Indian Mutiny.
India Bill – government of India passes from East India Company to the Crown.
Russia: Treaty of Aigun – gains the Amur region from China.
China: Treaties of Tientsin open 11 Chinese ports to western trade.

1860 China: Anglo-French force occupies Peking and burns the summer palace.

1862 China: French establish protectorate over Cochin-. China.

1863 French establish a protectorate over Cambodia.

1864 Expedition of British, Dutch, French and Americans bombard Shimonoseki, Japan.

1864–1880 Russia conquers Turkestan.

1868–1912 Meiji period in Japan – ends the anti-foreign policy.

MEDICINE

Florence Nightingale – the 'Lady with the Lamp' – revolutionized nursing during the Crimean War.

Joseph Lister's carbolic acid sprayer was used as an antiseptic during operations from 1875.

At the military hospital in the Crimea, Florence Nightingale, against much opposition, introduced new rules of cleanliness and hygiene and ensured that the wounded were properly cared for. On her return to England she raised money to found a proper nurses' school at St Thomas's Hospital, London.

Various 19th-century medical instruments including a stethoscope, ophthalmoscope and a syringe.

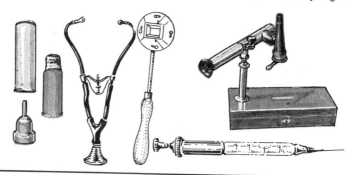

Africa was the last great region of the world to be brought under colonial control. Most of the continent was still independent when in 1884 Chancellor Bismarck of Germany called the Berlin conference. This laid down rules for the partition of Africa so as to avoid quarrels between the European powers. There followed one of the most remarkable power 'grabs' in history. Between 1884 and 1900 almost the entire continent was partitioned between the European powers. The only serious defeat they suffered was at Adowa in 1896 when the Ethiopians routed an Italian army.

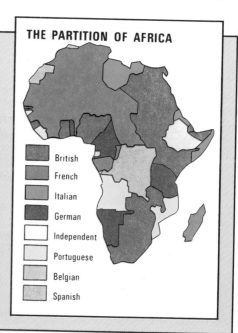

THE PARTITION OF AFRICA

- British
- French
- Italian
- German
- Independent
- Portuguese
- Belgian
- Spanish

EUROPE

1871 Britain legalizes trade unions.
Franco-Prussian War: Paris surrenders following 132-day siege. Commune set up in opposition to the national government and the peace terms. Government troops crush the Commune.
Treaty of Frankfurt officially ends the Franco-Prussian war – Alsace-Lorraine is ceded to Germany.
France has to pay an indemnity of 5000 million francs.
New German *Reich* (empire) is created with William of Prussia as its *Kaiser* (emperor) and Bismarck as chancellor.
1873–1874 First republic in Spain.
1874 Spanish monarchy restored.
1875 Disraeli, Britain's Prime Minister, purchases 42 per cent of the Suez Canal shares from Egypt.
Insurrection against Turkey by Herzegovina and Bosnia (now Yugoslavia) – annexed by Austria in 1908.
1876 Bulgarian 'atrocities' – thousands massacred by Turks following insurrection.
Serbia and Montenegro (now Yugoslavia) declare war on Turkey but are defeated.
1877 Russia and Turkey at war in the Balkans.
1878 Treaty of San Stefano ends Russo-Turkish war – Turkey loses Montenegro, Serbia, Bulgaria and Romania who become independent.
1879 Irish Land League is formed by Stewart Parnell MP.
1882 Phoenix Park murders – Lord Frederick Cavendish, Chief Secretary for Ireland and the Under-Secretary, Thomas Burke murdered in Dublin.
1882–1914 Triple Alliance of Germany, Austria and Italy.
1883 Sickness insurance introduced in Germany.
1884 Third Reform Act passed in Britain.
Berlin Conference signals the partitioning of Africa.
1886 Prime minister Gladstone introduces the first Irish Home Rule bill – defeated.
1889 Georges Boulanger (former French war minister) plots against the Third Republic in France – flees.
1890 William II German emperor, dismisses his Chancellor, Otto von Bismarck.
1893 Gladstone reintroduces Home Rule for Ireland – defeated in House of Lords.
Independent Labour Party founded in Britain by Keir Hardie.
1894 Dreyfus affair in France – Alfred Dreyfus, a Jewish officer in the French army, convicted of treason (military secrets to Germany) and deported. Many people convinced of his innocence, campaign for a new trial. One of Dreyfus' accusers admitted forging documents. A new trial found Dreyfus guilty but reduced sentence. In 1906 an appeal court cleared him.
1894–1917 Nicholas II, last tsar of Russia.
1895 Massacre of Armenians, by Turks, in Constantinople.
1897 Greece and Turkey at war over Crete.
1899 First Hague peace conference aims to settle international disputes peacefully.
1900 German Navy Law calling for a massive increase in German sea power starts arms race with Britain.

AFRICA & AMERICA

1876 Battle of Little Big Horn – Sioux Indians beat General Custer and his men.
1879 British-Zulu war in South Africa – Zulus are defeated.
1881 President James Garfield is assassinated.
Battle of Majuba Hill – Boers defeat British.
1882 British fleet bombards Alexandria and British occupy Cairo to suppress nationalists. French withdraw from Egypt.
Anti-Egyptian revolt in Sudan is led by Muslim leader, Mahdi Muhammad Ahmed.
1884 British General Gordon sent to rescue Egyptian garrisons in Sudan – besieged in Khartoum by Mahdi.
1886 Gold is discovered in South Africa.
1889 Brazil becomes a republic.
Cecil Rhodes founds British South Africa Company.
Panama scandal – collapse of Panama Canal Company.
Durand Agreement settles north-west frontier of India with Afghanistan.
1895–1896 War between Italy and Ethiopia.
1895–1896 Jameson Raid.
1895–1898 Cuban revolt against Spanish rule.
1896 Treaty of Addis Ababa – Italy recognises the independence of Ethiopia.
1898 Battle of Omdurman – British General Kitchener defeats the Sudanese.
Fashoda incident – confrontation between British and French in Sudan.
USA and Spain at war over Cuba.
Treaty of Paris – Cuba gains independence; Spain cedes Puerto Rico, Guam and the Philippines to the USA.
1899–1902 Boer War in South Africa.

MACHINES AT HOME

A London electric tram of 1890. Trams provided the first cheap and reliable form of transport in cities.

This horse omnibus of 1880 could carry 40 passengers and cost a shilling (5 pence) for six kilometres.

Mirror and basin combination installed in bathrooms at the end of the 19th century (top left) and the older type of movable bath. Water for the bath above was heated by a paraffin stove. Above: A pedestal water closet, 1888.

THE RUSSIAN REVOLUTION

Three revolutions shook Russia in the first years of the 20th century: in 1905 and in March and November 1917. Huge Russian war losses, bad government and terrible food shortages sparked off the March revolution. The tsar abdicated and a moderate provisional government was set up. But the Bolsheviks, a radical left-wing party, were determined to seize power. Their leader, V. I. Lenin returned from exile and in November the *Soviets* (workers' councils) under Leon Trotsky seized power. The new government centralized control of the land and food production and confiscated Church property.

Top: Oil stove, 1890.
Above: Electric hotplates, 1900.
A hand-operated suction cleaner.

1876 Korea opened to Japanese trade.
1877 Queen Victoria proclaimed 'Empress of India'.
1878–1880 Second Afghan war to prevent Russia gaining control. Britain gains control of Afghan affairs.
1885 New Guinea is divided between Britain and Germany. France establishes protectorates over Annam and Tonkin (Indochina).
1885–1886 Third Burmese war – Britain annexes upper Burma.
1889 New constitution in Japan leads to first general elections in 1890, though only a tiny minority has the vote.
1893–1906 Richard Seddon as Prime Minister of New Zealand introduces social reforms considered the most advanced in the world.
1893 Women's suffrage in New Zealand.
1894 China and Japan fight over Korea.
Sun Yat-sen founds first of several revolutionary societies in China.
1895 Treaty of Shimonoseki – Japan gains Formosa, China recognizes Korea's independence.
1896 Anglo-French agreement settles boundaries in Siam.
1898 China cedes Port Arthur to Russia.
USA annexes Hawaii.
Scramble for trading concessions by the European powers precipitates Boxer rebellion in China.
1900 Boxers, fanatical nationalists, attack Europeans and foreign legations.
Rebellion is suppressed by an international force of soldiers from Europe, Japan and USA. China forced to pay huge compensation.

FIRST WORLD WAR

1914 Jun 28: Assassination of the Archduke Ferdinand of Austria by a Bosnian student.
1914–1918 World War I: major Allied powers Britain, France, Russia, Italy, the USA – Central powers Germany, Austria-Hungary, Turkey.
1914 Jul 28: Austria invades Serbia.
Aug 4: Germans attack Belgium.
Aug 26: Battle of Tannenburg – Germans defeat the Russians.
Sept 5–9: Battle of Marne – Allies halt German advance on Paris.
Sept 6–15: Battle of Masurian Lakes – Russians retreat from East Prussia.
Oct 30–Nov 24: Battle of Ypres – the German push to the Channel ports is halted.
Trench warfare on the western and eastern fronts lasts to 1918.
Irish Home Rule Act – passed, separate Parliament in Ireland, some MPs at Westminster; position of Ulster (N. Ireland) to be decided.
1915 Jan 5: Britain announces naval blockade of Germany.
Gallipoli campaign – Allies land on Gallipoli peninsula, Turkey, but fail to win Dardanelles Straits from Turks (to 1916).
Feb 18: German submarine blockade of Britain.
Apr 22–May 25: Second battle of Ypres – Germans use poison gas for first time.
May 7: Sinking of British liner, *Lusitania*, by German U-boat – many civilians including Americans drowned.
Sept: Offensive by Britain and France – battles of Artois, Champagne, Loos – fails.
1916 Feb 21: Battle of Verdun begins German offensive on western front – continues to July, terrible losses and the stalemate continues.
Apr 24: Easter Rising in Ireland suppressed after a week.
May 31: Battle of Jutland – the only major naval battle of the war between Britain and Germany – indecisive.
Jul 1: Battle of the Somme to Nov 18 – British offensive, over one million killed. Britain uses tanks for first time.
Dec 7: British prime minister, Lloyd George forms War Cabinet.
1917 February Revolution in Russia – Tsar Nicholas II abdicates; a provisional government set up.
Apr 6: USA declares war on Germany.
Jul 31: Third battle of Ypres (Passchendaele) – a major Allied offensive, German counter-attack, few gains.
Oct 24: Battle of Caporetto – Italians defeated.
Nov 6–Nov 7: October Revolution – Bolsheviks led by Lenin seize power in Russia.
Nov 8: Balfour Declaration – Britain announces support for a Jewish state in Palestine.
1918 Mar 3: Treaty of Brest-Litovsk between Russia and Germany – Russia withdraws from war.
Women over 30 get the vote in Britain.
Jul 15–Aug 2: Second battle of the Marne – the last major German offensive – fails.
Jul: Tsar Nicholas and family are murdered.
Aug 8: Allied offensive on western front breaks through the Hindenburg line of defences – Germans retreat.
Oct 24: Battle of Vittorio Veneto – Italian victory – Austria-Hungary surrenders.
German navy mutinies, Kaiser William II abdicates.
Nov 11: Armistice and World War I ends.

EUROPE

1903 Women's Social and political Union formed in Britain by the Suffragette, Mrs. Emmeline Pankhurst.
1904 *Entente cordiale* between Britain and France.
1905 End of union between Sweden and Norway.
'Bloody Sunday' in St Petersburg – Russian troops fire on workers, 500 killed.
1912 *Titanic* liner sinks – 1513 die.
First Balkan War – Bulgaria, Greece, Serbia and Montenegro unite against Turkey, Balkans victorious.
1913 Third Irish Home Rule Bill passes the British House of Commons but is rejected by the Lords.
Second Balkan War – Serbia, Greece, Romania and Turkey unite against Bulgaria. Macedonia is divided up between Greece and Serbia.
1919 Jan: Peace conference begins in Paris. Founding of the League of Nations.
June: Treaty of Versailles is signed by Germany – it loses Alsace-Lorraine and colonies and has to pay allies reparation.
Sept: Treaty of Saint-Germain is signed by Austria – end of Habsburg monarchy.
Austria recognizes independence of Czechoslovakia, Poland, Yugoslavia and Hungary.
1920 Civil War in Ireland – made worse by the British auxiliaries, the Black and Tans. Ireland partitioned into north and south.
Poles repel Russian invasion.
Nov: Final collapse of counter-revolution in Russia.
Soviet government accepts existence of the newly-made border countries and makes treaties with them.

ELSEWHERE

1904 Tibet: Sir Francis Young-husband leads an expedition from India – treaty opens Tibet to western (British) trade.
1904–1905 Russo-Japanese War over rival ambitions in Korea and Manchuria.
1905 Russo-Japanese War – Port Arthur, China, falls to Japan.
Battle of Mukden – Russians defeated by Japanese.
Battle of Tsushima – Russian fleet destroyed by Japanese.
India: Partition of Bengal favours Muslims and raises strong nationalist feelings.
1906 Morocco: Algeciras Conference – Germany recognizes France's rights.
USA: Severe earthquake in San Francisco.
1908 Africa: Belgian government takes over the Congo Free State from the king because of inadequacy of his rule.
1909 American explorer Robert Peary reaches North Pole.
US manufacturer Henry Ford begins assembly line production of motor cars.
1911 China: Sun Yat-sen leads revolution and overthrows weak Manchu dynasty to form a republic (1912).
Norwegian explorer Roald Amundsen reaches South Pole.
1912 Africa: France establishes a protectorate in Morocco – the Spanish zone is defined.
Africa: Treaty of Ouchy ends the Italian-Turkish war – Turkey cedes Tripoli to Italy.
1919 India: Mohandas (Mahatma) Gandhi begins campaign of passive resistance against British.
Amritsar massacre – British troops fire on rioters.
1920 Palestine established as Jewish state under British administration.
USA: Prohibition to 1933.

NEW COMMUNICATIONS

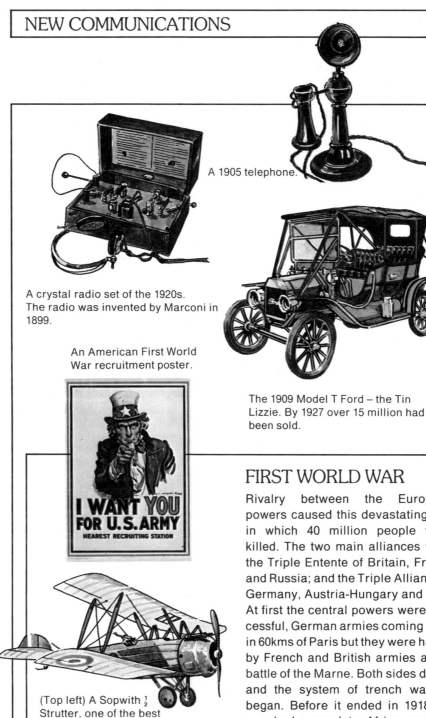

A 1905 telephone.

A crystal radio set of the 1920s. The radio was invented by Marconi in 1899.

An American First World War recruitment poster.

I WANT YOU FOR U.S. ARMY
NEAREST RECRUITING STATION

The 1909 Model T Ford – the Tin Lizzie. By 1927 over 15 million had been sold.

(Top left) A Sopwith $\frac{1}{2}$ Strutter, one of the best light bombers of the First World War.

The British Mark IV tank of 1917.

FIRST WORLD WAR

Rivalry between the European powers caused this devastating war in which 40 million people were killed. The two main alliances were the Triple Entente of Britain, France and Russia; and the Triple Alliance of Germany, Austria-Hungary and Italy. At first the central powers were successful, German armies coming within 60kms of Paris but they were halted by French and British armies at the battle of the Marne. Both sides dug in and the system of trench warfare began. Before it ended in 1918 the war had spread to Africa and the Middle East. In 1917 Russia made peace with Germany but the USA entered the war on the side of the Triple Entente and its enormous resources tipped the balance against the central powers. Many new weapons were used during this war, the most important being poison gas, the tank and the aeroplane.

EUROPE

1921 Irish Free State established.
Irish Republican Army (IRA) continues opposition.
Greece attacks Turkey and is defeated in 1922.
1922 Fascists march on Rome – King Victor Emmanuel asks Benito Mussolini to be prime minister.
USSR established.
Mustafa Kemal deposes the sultan of Turkey.
1923 Adolf Hitler, founder of the National Socialist (Nazi) Party in Germany attempts to overthrow Bavarian government, but is imprisoned.
Turkey proclaims itself a republic – first president Mustafa Kemal (Atatürk).
1924 First Labour government in Britain.
Death of Lenin – succeeded by Joseph Stalin.
1926 General Strike in Britain.
Portuguese government overthrown by army.
Germany is admitted to the League of Nations.
1930 London naval conference – great powers fail to agree upon naval limitations.
1931 Statute of Westminster defines status of British Dominions.
Commonwealth of Nations replaces 'British Empire'.
Financial crisis splits the British Labour government – formation of the Coalition National Government.
King Alfonso XIII of Spain flees the country – republic is proclaimed.
1932 Portuguese Finance Minister Antonio de Oliveira Salazar, becomes dictator of Portugal.
1933 President Hindenburg of Germany appoints Adolf Hitler chancellor.
Burning of the German *Reichstag* (parliament).
Germany withdraws from League of Nations.
National Socialists (Nazis) begin to eliminate all opposition and gain control in Germany.
Stalin purges the Communist Party in Russia.
Spanish government suppresses Anarchists in Barcelona.

ELSEWHERE

1921–1922 Washington Conference to discuss naval armaments – Pacific Treaty between Britain, France, Japan and USA.
1922 Egypt declared independent of British and French influence.
1923 Ethiopia admitted to the League of Nations.
1924 China: Sun Yat-sen establishes government including Communists at Guangz Hoo.
1925–1926 Africa: Arab uprising in Morocco led by Abd-el-Krim crushed by France and Spain.
1926 Australia: Canberra becomes the federal capital.
1927 Charles Lindbergh (US) makes first solo flight across the Atlantic.
China: Chiang Kai-shek (successor to Sun Yat-sen) purges Communists – sets up government at Nanjing.
Civil war follows between Communists and Nationalists.
1929 US stock market collapses leading to worldwide economic depression.
Palestine: First major conflict between Jews and Arabs.
1930 Africa: Ras Tafari crowned as Haile Selassie I of Ethiopia.
1931 Japanese occupy Manchuria.
1932 Canada: Imperial Conference at Ottawa – Britain gives trade preferences to her Commonwealth.
USA: 12 million Americans unemployed.
1932–1935 S. America: Paraguay and Bolivia at war over the Chaco region.
1933 USA: End of Prohibition.
1933–1936 USA: Roosevelt becomes president on campaign to introduce reforms known as the 'New Deal', to bring USA out of the depression.

MASS MARKET

The first supermarket was opened in New York in 1930.

Walt Disney's Micky Mouse first appeared in 1928.

Left: Telex machine of 1931.

EUROPE

1934 Nazis kill the Austrian chancellor, Dollfuss.
Death of President Hindenburg – Hitler becomes
Führer, leader of Germany.
1935 Hitler renounces the Treaty of Versailles –
declares a policy of rearmament for Germany.
Nuremburg Laws – persecution of Jews begins in
Germany.
Restoration of monarchy in Greece.
1936 Edward VIII, king of Britain, abdicates to marry
Mrs Simpson.
Germany reoccupies Rhineland.
Military revolt by General Francisco Franco against
the left-wing Republican government begins the
Spanish Civil War.
Italy and Germany support the Fascist Spanish
rebels under Franco and use the war to test
weapons and men in the field. USSR sends aid to
the Spanish Republicans.
Oct 25: Agreement between Italy and Germany
leads to the Rome-Berlin Axis.
1937 Apr 26: German planes bomb Guernica,
Spain.
May 28: Neville Chamberlain forms government in
Britain and favours a policy of appeasement
against Hitler.
1938 Mar 13: Germany annexes Austria.
Sept 29: Munich Pact between Hitler's Germany,
Mussolini's Italy, Chamberlain of Britain and
Daladier of France. Germany gains Sudetenland in
Czechoslovakia.
1939 Jan 26: Franco's nationalists capture
Barcelona.
Mar 10: Germany annexes Czechoslovakia.
Apr 1: Madrid surrenders – end of the Spanish Civil
War. Franco becomes dictator of Spain.
Apr 7: Italy invades Albania.
Sept 1: Germany invades Poland – beginning of
World War II.

ELSEWHERE

1934 China: Mao Zedong leads Communists
northwards on the Long March from Kiangsi – they
reach Yennan in 1935.
1935 Africa: Italian forces invade Ethiopia and the
League of Nations fails to intervene effectively.
Persia changes name to Iran.
India: Government of India Act passed by British
Parliament – sets up provincial councils.
1936 Africa: Italians take Addis Ababa and annex
Ethiopia.
1937 Africa: Anglo-Egyptian Treaty – British forces
in Egypt are restricted to the Suez Canal zone.
Treaty to last for 20 years.
China: July 7 – Japanese invade, capture Shanghai
and Beijing.

THE RISE OF FASCISM

A period of bitterness between the left and right of
politics followed the First World War. The fascists under
Benito Mussolini came to power in Italy in 1922. In
Germany the Weimar Republic failed to solve the
country's economic problems and by 1932 six million
Germans were unemployed. Hitler and his Nazi
(National Socialist) Party came to power in 1933,
suppressed all other parties and began persecuting the
Jews. In 1936 a civil war broke out in Spain between the
left-wing republican government and the right-wing
parties supported by the army and the Church. It cost
600,000 lives before General Francisco Franco and the
Falangists won power. Thus by 1939 three of the major
powers of Europe had fascist governments.

Left: The Short Sunderland flying boat
of 1938.
Above: After two terrible disasters
airships had, by 1938, fallen out of
favour.

A fashion-plate of the 1930s.

EUROPE

1939 Sept 1: Germany invades Poland.
Sept 3: Britain and France declare war on Germany.
Sept 17: Russia invades Poland.
Sept 29: Nazi-Soviet Pact – Poland partitioned between two powers.
Russo-Finnish war – Finland defeated in Nov 1940.
1940 Apr 9: Germany invades Denmark and Norway.
May 10: Germany invades Belgium, the Netherlands.
May 17: Germany invades France.
May 27: British army evacuated from Dunkirk.
Jun 10: Italy declares war on Britain and France.
Jun 14: Germans occupy Paris, France surrenders.
Jul 10–Oct 31: Battle of Britain – British air victory because Germany fails to concentrate attack on RAF bases.
Oct 28: Italy invades Greece.
1941 Jun 22: Germany invades Russia.
Leningrad besieged by Germans – relieved in January 1944.
Dec: Russian counter-offensive in the Ukraine.
1942 Sept 6: Battle of Stalingrad – Germans defeated.
1943 Sept 3: Italian government surrenders.
1944 Jun 4: Allies enter Rome.
Jun 6: Allies land in Normandy ('D-Day') – German retreat.
Jul 20: Bomb plot to assassinate Hitler fails.
Sept 2: Allies liberate Paris and Brussels.
Oct 3: Warsaw rising is crushed by Germans.
1945 Jan 17: Russians capture Warsaw.
Feb 7: Yalta Conference in Crimea – Churchill, Roosevelt and Stalin discuss post-war settlements.
Mar 7: Allies invade Germany.
Apr 28: Mussolini assassinated by Italian partisans.
Apr 30: Hitler commits suicide.
May 7: Germany surrenders.
May 8: 'VE Day' (victory in Europe).
Potsdam Conference – Allies discuss post-war settlements.
1946 League of Nations formally ended.
Nuremberg trials – Nazi leaders sentenced by the international court for war crimes.
1947 Allied peace treaties signed in Paris with Italy, Romania, Hungary, Bulgaria and Finland.
Marshall Aid – programme of aid for European recovery introduced by the US Secretary of State, George Marshall.
1948 Communist coup in Czechoslovakia.
1948–1949 USSR blockades Berlin – Allies 'airlift' supplies.

ASIA & THE PACIFIC

1940 Apr 30: Japan joins Axis powers (Germany-Italy).
1941 Dec 7: Japan attacks the US Pacific fleet in Pearl Harbor, Hawaii.
Dec 25: Japan takes Hong Kong.
1942 Jan: Japan captures Manila, Singapore, Rangoon, Mandalay and the Philippines.
1942 Jul 1: USA begins to recapture Pacific islands held by Japan.
1944 Oct 25: Battle of Leyte Gulf – defeat of Japanese navy by USA.
1945 Aug 6: First atomic bomb dropped on Hiroshima, Japan.
Aug 9: Second atomic bomb dropped on Nagasaki, Japan.
Aug 14: Japan surrenders – World War II ends.
1946 Transjordan (Jordan) becomes independent of Great Britain.
1946–1954 Civil War in Indochina between Vietnamese Nationalists under Ho Chi Minh and the French.
1947 Cheribon Agreement between the Dutch and Indonesia leads to the establishment of the United States of Indonesia.
India gains independence – two dominions are created; India (Hindu) and Pakistan (Muslim).
Partition of Palestine into Arab and Jewish states is agreed by UN but rejected by Arabs.
1948 State of Israel is declared.
Burma independent.
1948–1949 War between Israel and the Arab League.
1948 Assassination of Mahatma Gandhi by a Hindu extremist in India.
Ceylon independent as a dominion in the Commonwealth.
China split by conflict between Communists and Nationalists.
Korea is divided into Republic of Korea (south) and Communist People's Republic (North).

ELSEWHERE

1941 Dec 8: USA declares war on Axis powers.
1941 Egypt: Sept 1 – Germany and Italy invade.
1942 Egypt: Oct 23 – Battle of El Alamein – British defeat Germans. Germans retreat from north Africa. Anglo-American forces take Tripoli and Tunis.
1943 N. Africa: May – end of Axis resistance.
1949 South African government adopts policy of *apartheid* (separate development for blacks and whites).

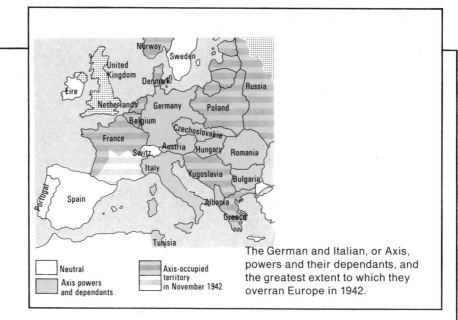

Neutral

Axis powers and dependants

Axis-occupied territory in November 1942

The German and Italian, or Axis, powers and their dependants, and the greatest extent to which they overran Europe in 1942.

SECOND WORLD WAR

Fifty million people were killed and 34 million wounded in this terrible war. It began with the German invasion of Poland on 1 September, 1939. The war was fought in four main theatres: Europe, Asia, Africa and the sea. At first the Germans overran most of Europe. Then in 1941 they turned east and attacked the USSR. They almost took Moscow before Russian resistance and bitter winter conditions turned back their armies. On 7 December 1941, Japan entered the war, attacking the American fleet in Pearl Harbor, an act which brought the USA into the war on the Allied side. From Africa allied forces invaded Italy in 1943 and then in June 1944 a huge allied army invaded France from Britain. By April 1945 the western allied armies met the Russians on the Elbe in the heart of Germany which surrendered on 7 May. The first nuclear (atomic) bombs were dropped on Japan in August 1945 forcing it to surrender.

The German fighter plane the Messerschmitt Bf109.

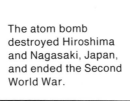

Mitsubishi Zero-Sen

War in the Pacific was started on 7 December, 1941 when Japanese planes bombed the American naval base at Pearl Harbor, Hawaii.

The atom bomb destroyed Hiroshima and Nagasaki, Japan, and ended the Second World War.

85

EUROPE

1949 North Atlantic Treaty Organization (NATO) is formed as a western defensive alliance.
Germany is divided into the Federal Republic (West) and Democratic Republic (East).
1952 Bonn Convention – Britain, France and the USA end the occupation of West Germany.
Greece and Turkey join NATO.
1953 Death of Stalin – Georgi Malenkov becomes Soviet prime minister.
Marshal Tito becomes president of Yugoslavia.
1954 Growth of demands for *enosis* – the union of Greece and Cyprus – leads to disturbances on the island.
1955 Formation of Warsaw Pact – treaty between East European Communist powers to oppose NATO.
EOKA, Greek Cypriot organization led by Grivas, begins anti-British terrorist activities in Cyprus.
West Germany is admitted to NATO.
1956 Khrushchev, new Soviet prime minister, denounces Stalin.
Anti-Russian uprising in Hungary crushed by Soviet forces.
1957 Treaty of Rome establishes the European Economic Community – the EEC or Common Market – (Belgium, France, West Germany, Italy, Luxembourg and Holland).
1958 Charles de Gaulle returns to power as first president of the French Fifth Republic.
1960 Cyprus becomes an independent republic under Archbishop Makarios.

ASIA

1949 Mao Zedong establishes Communist regime throughout China – Nationalist government escapes to Formosa (Taiwan).
France recognizes independent Vietnam and Cambodia.
Arab-Israeli peace and the partition of Jerusalem.
USSR recognizes the People's Republic of China.
1950–1953 Korean War – North Korea supported by China, South Korea by UN force.
1951 Chinese forces occupy Tibet.
Colombo Plan for economic development of south and south-east Asia comes into effect.
1952 First national elections in India – Jawaharlal Nehru becomes prime minister.
1953 Hillary and Tenzing, first men to reach the top of Everest, the world's highest mountain.
Treaty of Panmunjon ends Korean War.
French forces occupy Dien Bien Phu, North Vietnam – Viet Minh forces invade Laos.
1954 French are defeated at Dien Bien Phu.
Geneva Conference: Vietnam is divided – North Vietnam under Ho Chi Minh (Communist) and South Vietnam with the support of the USA and Britain.
Beginning of the Vietnam war as the Communists of the north try to take over the south.
Formation of South-East Asia Treaty Organization (SEATO) to prevent the spread of Communism in south-east Asia.
1958 Egypt and Syria form the United Arab Republic (UAR) later joined by Yemen to form the United Arab States.
Abdul Kassem leads military revolt in Iraq – King Faisal II is assassinated.
1959 Uprising against the Chinese in Tibet – Dalai Lama flees to India, the revolt is crushed.

END OF EMPIRES

An important development in the period after the Second World War was the rapid dismantling of the European empires in Asia and Africa. In 1945 only 51 countries formed the new United Nations; 40 years later it had more than 150 members and most of the new states had been colonies. The British Indian Empire became independent in 1947 and the Dutch East Indies (Indonesia) at the same time. Then in the 1950s and 1960s most of the remaining colonial territories of Africa, the West Indies and the Pacific became independent. The importance of this change from empires controlled by a few European powers to many independent countries has been immense: it created what we have come to call the Third World.

Mao Zedong, the Chairman of China's Communist party, united the country in 1949.

1951 Egypt withdraws from Anglo-Egyptian Agreement on Suez Canal – British troops occupy Canal Zone.
1952 Kenya: Mau Mau (secret nationalist organization) begins terrorist activities against British.
Egypt: Coup ousts King Farouk – army, led nominally by General Neguib, takes over – real power is Colonel Nasser.
1953 Kenya: Trial and imprisonment of Jomo Kenyatta on charge of directing Mau Mau.
1956 Suez: Britain withdraws troops from Canal Zone.
Egypt: Colonel Gamal Abdel Nasser elected president. Nasser nationalizes the Suez Canal.
Israeli forces invade Egypt. Anglo-French forces invade and occupy the Canal Zone – an international crisis follows. UN calls for cease-fire and sends in emergency forces to enforce it.
1959 Cuba: Overthrow of Batista's government – Fidel Castro becomes president.
1960 By now 20 African colonies are independent.
USA: J. F. Kennedy elected president.

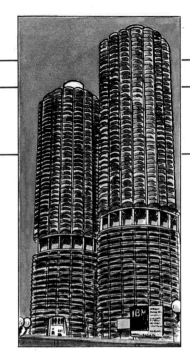

Goldberg's Marina City in Chicago, USA. Cars are parked at the bottom, offices are in the middle, and flats are at the top.

The Modulo was built by Pininfarina of Italy in 1969.

The Harrier GR1, the world's first vertical take-off warplane, 1969.

Concorde can travel at twice the speed of sound. It is a masterpiece of supersonic design.

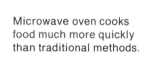

Microwave oven cooks food much more quickly than traditional methods.

A French train designed for very high speeds. It has gas turbine engines.

Non-stick frying pans were developed in the 1950s.

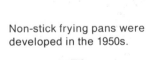

The North American Greyhound bus company provides cheap and fast travel all over the USA.

EUROPE & AMERICA

1961 Berlin Wall is built.
Nuclear test ban treaty signed by Britain, USA and USSR.
Bay of Pigs – abortive invasion of Castro's Cuba by American-backed Cuban exiles.
1962 President Kennedy of the USA demands that the Russians remove missiles and bombers from Cuba. Faced with threat of war, Russia agrees.
Telstar communications satellite launched – first live TV broadcasts between USA and Europe.
1963 Assassination of US President Kennedy in Dallas.
1964 Fighting between Greek and Turkish communities in Cyprus.
Civil Rights Act becomes law in USA.
Soviet leader Khrushchev succeeded by Alexei Kosygin.
1965 Britain abolishes death penalty for murder.
1966 French president De Gaulle vetoes the second British application to join the EC.
1967 Military coup in Greece.
1968 Soviet troops invade Czechoslovakia to crush liberalism of Czech leader Alexander Dubcek.
Death of Salazar, Portuguese dictator since 1933.
Student demonstrations in Paris.
USA: Assassination of black civil rights leader Martin Luther King and presidential candidate Robert Kennedy.
1969 American astronauts – Neil Armstrong and 'Buzz' Aldrin – land on moon.
1970 US President Richard Nixon announces the invasion of Cambodia.
1972 Britain assumes direct rule in Ulster.
Britain, Denmark and Ireland join the EC.
Greek military junta in Athens resigns.
1973 US-backed military coup in Chile overthrows Marxist President Salvador Allende, who is killed.
1974 President Nixon is forced to resign over Watergate scandal – he is succeeded by Vice President Gerald Ford.
1975 Spanish dictator Franco dies. Juan Carlos, grandson of last king of Spain, becomes king.
1976 Jimmy Carter wins US Presidential election.
1978 USA establishes diplomatic relations with Communist China, ends those with Taiwan.
1979 53 Americans held hostage by Islamic students in Iran.

ASIA

1962 Border clashes between China and India.
1963 South Vietnamese government overthrown by military coup.
1964 Increased US involvement in Vietnam.
US declares support for South Vietnam against the Communist Vietcong.
1964–1966 War between Malaysia and Indonesia.
1965 US begins regular bombing raids against North Vietnam.
War between India and Pakistan over Kashmir – UN calls for ceasefire.
1966 End of war between Malaysia and Indonesia.
'Cultural Revolution' in China (to 1968).
1967 Six-Day War (June 5–10) between Arabs and Israel.
1968 Vietcong launch major offensive in Vietnam.
1970 Civil war in Jordan between government troops and Palestine guerrillas.
1971 East Pakistan breaks away from Pakistan to form new state of Bangladesh.
Communist China joins the UN; Taiwan is expelled.
1972 Ceylon changes name to Sri Lanka.
1973 USA withdraws troops from Vietnam – peace settlement signed in Paris.
October *(Yom Kippur)* War – Arab states attack Israel, ceasefire after five weeks.
Arab oil-producing states cut oil supplies, raise the price and start world economic crisis.
1975 Communist victories in Cambodia.
South Vietnam surrenders to North Vietnam: end of Vietnam War.
1976 Death of China's leaders Chou en-Lai and Mao Zedong.
1977 President Sadat of Egypt goes to Israel on peace mission – Prime Minister Begin of Israel returns the visit and two countries negotiate.
1978 UN force is sent to Lebanon to police border with Israel.
1979 Egypt and Israel sign a peace treaty.

AFRICA

1960 Civil War follows independence in the Congo as Katanga Province under Moise Tshombe attempts to secede.
1961 Murder of Congo's prime minister Patrice Lumumba. South Africa becomes Republic and withdraws from Commonwealth.
1962 Algeria becomes independent of France after eight years at war.
1963 Organization of African Unity (OAU) is formed by independent African states.
1965 Ian Smith and white Rhodesian minority government make Unilateral Declaration of Independence (UDI) from Britain.
1966 Assassination of South African prime minster, Dr. Verwoerd – succeeded by John Vorster.
1967–1970 Nigerian civil war – Biafra tries and fails to break away from Nigeria.
1974 Independence for all Portuguese African territories is recognized.
1976 Soweto riots in South Africa.
1979 Amin flees Uganda in face of invasion by exiled Ugandans supported by Tanzanian army.
New constitution for Rhodesia – Britain takes control again.

THE NEW TECHNOLOGY

Xerox machine. Documents can be copied quickly and cheaply in the office.

The electronic calculator was invented in 1971. It can do the most complicated calculation in moments.

The invention of the microprocessor, basically an entire computer on a single silicon chip, revolutionized the computer industry.

THE SPACE AGE

The space age began in 1957 when the Russians launched Sputnik I, the first artificial earth satellite. Then the USA launched Explorer I and the two superpowers engaged in a space race. In 1961 the Russians sent the first man, Yuri Gagarin, into space. In 1969 the Americans reached the Moon and 600 million television viewers on Earth saw Neil Armstrong walk on its surface. By 1986 the spacecraft Voyager 2 was sending pictures of Uranus back to Earth.

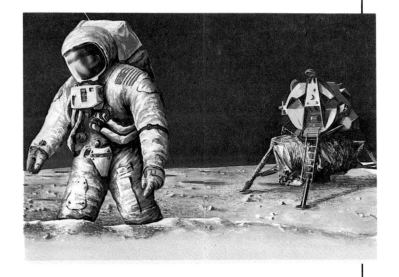

Astronauts exploring the Moon. The first astronauts on the Moon were Neil Armstrong and Edwin Aldrin in 1969.

EUROPE & AMERICA

1980 Death of President Tito of Yugoslavia.
Assassination attempt on Pope John Paul II.
1981 Ronald Reagan becomes US president.
Assassination attempt on President Reagan.
1982 Argentina invades Falkland Islands. British
taskforce reoccupies the islands.
President Brezhnev of USSR dies.
1983 Yuri Andropov becomes leader of the USSR.
US invasion of the Caribbean island of Grenada.
1984 The Soviet leader, Andropov, dies; succeeded
by Konstantin Chernenko.
The Sandinistas win overwhelming victory in the
first elections in Nicaragua since the overthrow of
the Somoza government in 1979.
1985 Death of Soviet leader Chernenko; he is
succeeded by Mikhail Gorbachev.
US supplies aid to the Contra rebels in Nicaragua.
Eruption of Nevada del Ruiz volcano (dormant for
400 years) in Colombia kills 25,000.
1986 Spain and Portugal join the European
Community.
Nuclear accident at Chernobyl in the USSR.
Voyager aircraft flies non-stop round the world
without refuelling.
1987 US-USSR treaty to eliminate land-based
medium range nuclear missiles.
1988 George Bush is elected president of the USA.
1989 US space probe Voyager 2 flies within 4800 km
of planet Neptune.
Communist rule ends in East Germany; the Berlin
Wall is demolished.
End of the Cold War as from December 3.
Communist rule ends in Bulgaria, Czechoslovakia,
Hungary and Romania.
1990 Lithuania declares its independence.
Communist rule ends in Albania.
West and East Germany are united.
Britain's Prime Minister, Margaret Thatcher,
resigns: John Major succeeds her.
1991 Boris Yeltsin becomes the first elected
president of the Russian Republic.
Civil war breaks out in Yugoslavia as Slovenia and
Croatia declare independence.
USSR: Attempt to overthrow President Gorbachev
fails; he later ends Communist rule there.
The 14 remaining republics of the USSR declare
their independence; the Soviet Union is dissolved.
1992 Conservatives under John Major win general
election in Britain with greatly reduced majority.
Yugoslavia breaks up as Bosnia/Herzegovina and
Macedonia declare independence; Serbs in Bosnia
kill and ill-treat Muslims.
Democrat William 'Bill' Clinton defeats Republican
George Bush in US presidential election.

ASIA

1980 War between Iran and Iraq.
1981 President Sadat of Egypt assassinated.
1982 Israel invades Lebanon and advances on
Beirut to drive PLO fighters from the country.
1983 Growing Sikh violence in the Punjab leads the
central government of India to take direct control.
1984 War between Iraq and Iran escalates.
Major economic reforms in China.
Indira Gandhi, Prime Minister of India is
assassinated.
At Bhopal in India 2500 people are killed following
a leak of toxic gas from a Union Carbide plant.
1985 Israel withdraws from Lebanon.
1987 Iran-Iraq war threatens oil shipments.
India sends troops to Sri Lanka to control Tamil
rebels.
Chairman Deng gives up all posts in China except
control of the army.
Portugal promises to return Macao to China.
1988 Iran-Iraq War ends after eight years.
1989 Last Soviet troops leave Afghanistan.
USSR and China resume diplomatic relations.
Burma becomes the Union of Myanmar.
Tianamen Square massacre in Beijing; thousands
of demonstrators calling for democracy are shot.
Pakistan rejoins the Commonwealth.
1990 Fighting breaks out between the Soviet
republics of Armenia and Azerbaijan.
The two Yemens unite as one country.
Earthquake in Iran kills 40,000 people.
Iraq invades Kuwait and declares it annexed.
1991 United Nations forces free Kuwait in an aerial
bombardment and a 100-hour land battle. Iraqis
torch Kuwait's oil wells as they leave.
India's prime minister Chandra Shekar resigns.
Former premier Rajiv Gandhi is assassinated.
Mount Pinatubo in the Philippines erupts.
China agrees to sign a nuclear weapons treaty.
Israel frees 91 Arab prisoners.
Middle East peace conference opens in Spain.
Cambodia's former ruler, Prince Norodom
Sihanouk, returns and becomes president.
Lebanese terrorists free the last British and
American hostages.
1992 Kurds in Iraq receive international help.
UN continues destruction of Iraqi weapons.
Pakistan's former prime minister, Benazir Bhutto,
is arrested on conspiracy charges.

Index

The abbreviations K. (King) and Q. (Queen) are used where appropriate. Illustrations and maps are indicated by page numbers in *italics*.

RACE TO THE MOON

EXPEDITION

THE STORY OF APOLLO 11

EXPEDITION

EDITOR APRIL McCROSKIE
Technical Advisor Mark Whitchurch

An SBC Book, created, designed and produced by
The Salariya Book Company
25 Marlborough Place
Brighton
East Sussex
BN1 1UB

First published in 1998 by Franklin Watts
96 Leonard Street London EC2A 4RH

Franklin Watts Australia
14 Mars Road Lane Cove NSW 2066

ISBN 0 7496 2766 2
Dewey Decimal Classification 629.45
A CIP catalogue record for this book is available
from the British Library.

JEN GREEN
graduated from the University of Sussex with a PhD in
English Literature in 1982. She has worked as an editor
and manager in children's publishing for 15 years and
is now a full-time writer. She has written many books
for children.
For Hannah and Edward, JG.

MARK BERGIN
was born in Hastings in 1961. He studied at
Eastbourne College of Art and has specialized in
historical reconstruction since leaving art school in
1983. He lives in Sussex with his wife and children.
For Hannah, Isabelle and Edward, MB.

DAVID SALARIYA
was born in Dundee, Scotland. He has designed and
created many new series of children's books. In 1989,
he established The Salariya Book Company Ltd.
He lives in Brighton with his wife, the illustrator
Shirley Willis, and their son Jonathan.

RACE TO THE MOON

The Story of Apollo 11

Written by JEN GREEN

Illustrated by MARK BERGIN

Created and designed by
DAVID SALARIYA

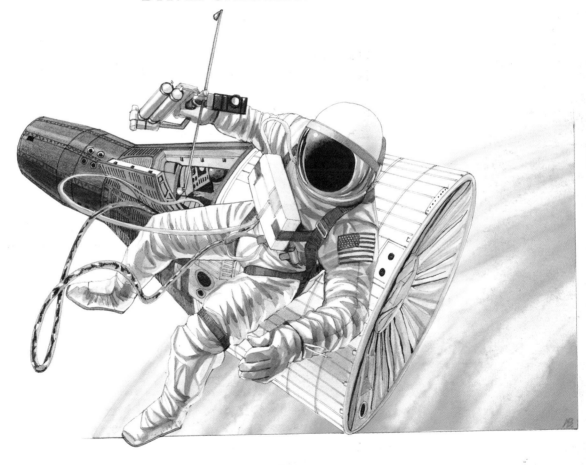

W

FRANKLIN WATTS
NEW YORK • LONDON • SYDNEY

CONTENTS

EYEWITNESS

INTRODUCTION

ONE MORNING in the late 20th century, a tiny silver spacecraft dropped from a black, star-filled sky towards the rocky surface of a minor planet. The craft drifted down slowly, and landed with a puff of dust. It rocked on its landing legs, then steadied. The craft and its occupants were quite alone in a vast, silent landscape pitted with deep-shadowed craters which stretched away in every direction.

A small hatch opened in the spacecraft. A figure dressed in a bulky suit climbed down the spaceship's ladder and stepped onto the grey, powdery surface. The date was 21 July 1969, and human beings had landed on the Moon. It was just twelve years since the first object made by humans had reached space, and a race to land on the Moon had begun. This brief period had seen enormous advances in science and technology – advances that paved the way for that historic landing on the Moon.

Note:
Where the Soviet Union is mentioned throughout the text, this refers to the former USSR.

5

•ROCKET POWER•

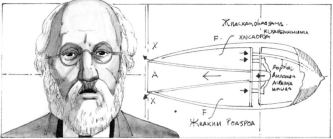

The First Rockets
Rockets were invented in China about 2,000 years ago. They were used as weapons against the Mongol army that invaded China in AD 1232. For the next 500 years rockets were used as fireworks and as weapons.

Tsiolkovsky's Idea
The father of modern space travel was Konstantin Tsiolkovsky, a Russian inventor. In 1903 he suggested that liquid fuel should be used to power rockets, since it could be controlled more easily than solid fuel.

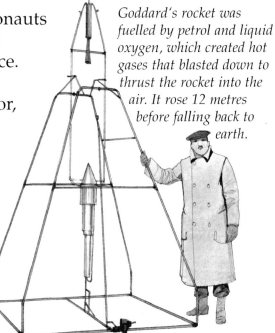

Goddard's rocket was fuelled by petrol and liquid oxygen, which created hot gases that blasted down to thrust the rocket into the air. It rose 12 metres before falling back to earth.

HUNDREDS OF YEARS before astronauts set foot on the Moon, a few people dreamed of travelling through space. But it was not until the early 20th century that a Russian inventor, Konstantin Tsiolkovsky, thought of using rockets to reach space. An American scientist, Robert Goddard, was the first to build and launch a successful rocket, in 1926.

During World War II, the German army used rockets to launch bombs under the supervision of a scientist named Wernher von Braun. After the war, von Braun went to live in America. He was to mastermind the American space programme, including the Apollo launches.

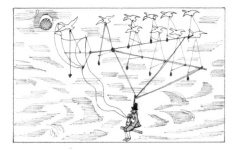

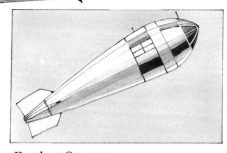

Space Dreams
In the 16th century, an author called Francis Godwin wrote a story about a trip to the Moon. The hero was towed there by a team of wild swans.

Science Fiction
In 1865 French author, Jules Verne, wrote a science fiction book about a journey to the Moon. His book inspired scientists such as von Braun.

Rocket Stages
Tsiolkovsky thought Earth's gravity could be overcome by using rockets, arranged in stages so they could take over from each other.

•DREAMS OF SPACE TRAVEL•

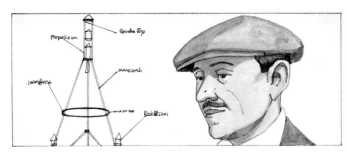

Goddard's Rocket

An American scientist, Robert Goddard, built the first high-altitude rocket in 1926. Like Tsiolkovsky, Goddard realized that only a rocket, which could carry all its own fuel, could escape Earth's gravity to reach space.

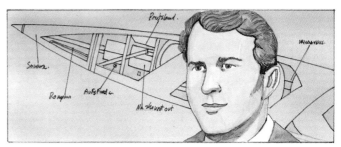

Vengeance Weapon

During World War II a scientist named Wernher von Braun developed a rocket-powered missile in Germany. It was called the V-2, or vengeance weapon.

During World War II Germany launched V-2 rockets carrying explosives. Over 1,400 rockets were fired at London. Following Tsiolkovsky's theory, they burned liquid fuel. When Germany was defeated in 1945, von Braun surrendered to the United States army and became an American citizen.

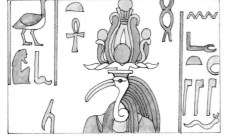

Moon Myths

For centuries star-gazers have marvelled at the Moon in the sky. To the ancient Egyptians, the Moon was the symbol of Thoth, god of wisdom.

Man in the Moon

Throughout history the craters on the Moon's surface suggested to people the shapes of animals such as a hare, or a giant human face.

Little Green Men

The idea that the Moon might be inhabited by aliens persisted well into the 20th century, and inspired many science fiction films.

•FIRST IN SPACE•

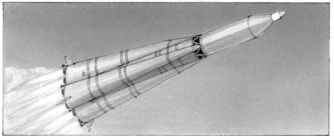

The Space Age Begins

The Soviet space programme was led by a brilliant scientist, Sergei Korolyev. By 1957 Soviets had built a powerful rocket, the SS-6. On 4 October the rocket was used to place a satellite, *Sputnik 1*, in orbit round the Earth.

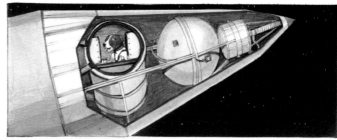

First Space Traveller

In November 1957 the Soviets followed this success with another impressive first. A second, larger satellite, *Sputnik 2*, carried a dog called Laika into space. Unfortunately Laika did not survive her trip.

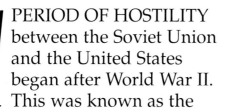

A PERIOD OF HOSTILITY between the Soviet Union and the United States began after World War II. This was known as the Cold War. The two countries wanted to show that their scientists were making great advances (and so would be capable of making new and terrible weapons). Americans believed that their technology was superior, so were shocked when the Soviets shot a satellite, *Sputnik 1*, into space. Soon a second triumph was announced: the Soviets had put a man, Yuri Gagarin in space.

A new powerful Soviet rocket was used to launch Gagarin into space. His spacecraft Vostok ("East") 1, was a round capsule on top of an instrument section with rockets which fired to control the craft's position.

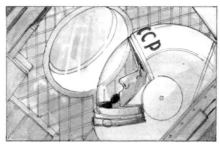

Gagarin's Flight

As he was blasted into the atmosphere in *Vostok 1*, Gagarin had a unique view of the Earth as it fell away beneath him.

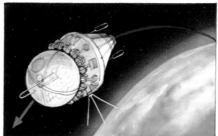

In Orbit

Vostok 1 orbited the Earth at over 27,000 kilometres an hour, flying over India, Australia and Africa. Then the spacecraft slowed for re-entry.

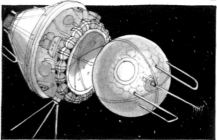

Re-Entry

As the re-entry sequence began, Gagarin's craft had to enter Earth's atmosphere at exactly the right speed and angle, to avoid burning up.

American Launch
American attempts to match the Soviets failed. After a navy rocket exploded on the launch pad, von Braun was called in to design America's rockets. In 1958 he launched the first American satellite, *Explorer 1.*

Man in Space
On 12 April 1961, after more test flights with dogs, the Soviets put the first man in space. Major Yuri Gagarin was the first "cosmonaut" – the Russian word for astronaut. He made a single orbit of the Earth.

A satellite is an object, natural or manufactured, orbiting (circling) another in space. The Moon is a satellite of the Earth. The first manufactured satellite, Sputnik 1, was a small metal sphere containing a radio transmitter. Long aerials were attached to the sphere, which weighed 84 kilograms, as much as a heavy person. Sputnik ("Traveller") orbited the Earth for 92 days before burning up.

Fireball
The capsule glowed with heat as it entered the atmosphere. Gagarin experienced powerful forces called G forces as his craft slowed down.

Ejection
Gagarin ejected at a height of 7,000 metres. At the time the Soviets claimed he had not ejected, to make the flight sound even more impressive.

Safe Landing
Gagarin's parachute brought him down to Earth near the River Volga in Russia. His craft also landed safely using parachutes.

•THE RACE BEGINS•

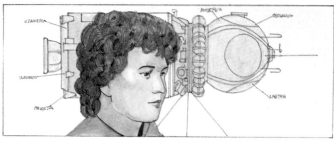

Americans in Space

In 1961 the first American astronaut, Alan Shepard, entered space. The following year John Glenn became the first American to orbit the Earth. He completed three circuits before splashing down in the Atlantic Ocean.

First Woman Cosmonaut

In 1963 the Soviets pressed forward again; Valentina Tereshkova became the first woman in space. She spent almost three days in space, completing 48 orbits. Her spacecraft liaised with another Soviet craft.

G AGARIN'S SUCCESS embarrassed the United States. America's National Aeronautics and Space Administration (NASA) had been formed in 1958: its aim was to put a man in space. By 1961 NASA had sent a chimpanzee named Ham on a brief space flight, but while von Braun was perfecting the American rocket, news came of Gagarin's success. In May 1961 the new president, John F. Kennedy, vowed that America would place a man on the Moon and return him safely to Earth before 1970. The race was on.

Following President Kennedy's speech in 1961, the Moon landing project, code-named Apollo, *was given massive funding.*

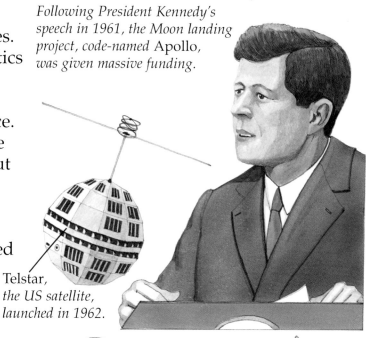

Telstar, *the US satellite, launched in 1962.*

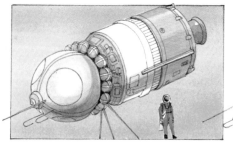

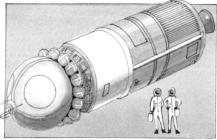

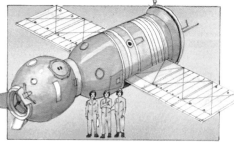

Soviet Spacecraft
1. Vostok
During the 1960s the Soviets developed three craft for use in space. *Vostok* was the first Soviet spacecraft.

2. Voskhod
By 1964 the Soviets had altered the design of *Vostok* to produce *Voskhod*, which could carry three cosmonauts in very cramped conditions.

3. Soyuz
The Soviets launched a new craft, *Soyuz* ("*Union*") in 1967. The first mission ended in disaster when the craft crashed after 18 orbits.

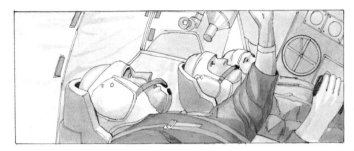

Cosmonauts in "Shirt-Sleeves"

In 1964 the Soviets launched *Voskhod 1* (*"Sunrise"*) which carried three cosmonauts in a cabin filled with air, so there was no need for spacesuits.

First Walk in Space

In 1965 Russian cosmonaut Alexei Leonov took the first "walk" in space. On re-entry his craft landed 3,200 kilometres off course and the crew had to spend a night surrounded by wolves before rescue came!

Leonov's space walk put the Soviets ahead again but the trip was not trouble-free. Leonov struggled to re-enter his craft because his spacesuit made it difficult for him to bend enough to fit back through the hatch. In June 1965, American astronaut Edward White (right) also walked in space, manoeuvring with gas jets from a hand-held gun.

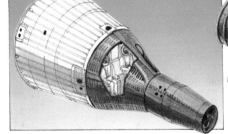

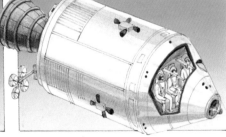

American Spacecraft

1. Mercury

The first American spaceships were *Mercury* capsules. They were used for space missions from 1961-3.

2. Gemini

Two-person *Geminis* replaced *Mercury* craft in 1965. Astronauts controlled the craft themselves and practised manoeuvring in space.

3. Apollo

Although the *Apollo* space programme began in 1963, the first *Apollo* craft did not get off the ground until 1968.

•AMERICA CATCHES UP•

Docking Practice
During 1965-9 American astronauts practised for the Moon mission in *Gemini* craft. Two *Apollo* craft would need to meet and dock (join) in space. In 1965 *Geminis* 5 and 6 flew within metres of each other.

Launch Pad Disaster
In 1967 the *Apollo* project was struck by disaster. Three astronauts died when fire broke out in their capsule on the launch pad. The materials used in the craft were quickly changed to make it less likely to catch fire.

SO, by the early 1960s, America and the Soviet Union were racing one another to the Moon. The *Apollo* spaceship designed by the Americans consisted of two craft which could fly together but also operate separately: a command ship and a Moon lander. The Moon lander would visit the Moon and then rejoin the main ship for the trip back to Earth. A new rocket would be needed to carry the craft into space. But there were questions about the Moon itself. Was the surface suitable for landing, or was it covered with a layer of dust which a spacecraft would sink into? Both countries sent unmanned craft, called probes, to investigate.

American probe, Surveyor 3.

"Phases" of the Moon
As the Moon orbits the Earth, we can see more or less of the side that is lit by the Sun. This makes the Moon appear to change shape.

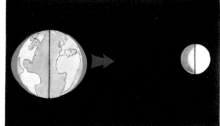

Force of Gravity
The pull of Earth's gravity on the Moon keeps it in orbit around us. The Moon's gravity pulls the oceans on our planet, causing tides.

Distant World
The Moon is 384,400 kilometres from Earth. It took *Apollo 8* three days to reach it, travelling at a top speed of 38,400 kilometres per hour.

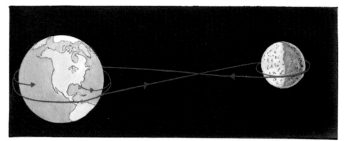

Apollo 8

In December 1968 *Apollo 8* lifted off on a mission vital to the programme. On board Frank Borman, Jim Lovell and Bill Anders were the first men to leave Earth's orbit and start travelling to the Moon.

Far Side of the Moon

The *Apollo 8* astronauts were the first to see the far side of the Moon, on Christmas Eve, 1968. The crew spent 20 hours orbiting the Moon before returning safely to Earth and splashing down in the Pacific Ocean.

On the Moon's far side, the crew of Apollo 8 lost contact with NASA when the bulk of the Moon blocked out radio signals. Everyone at Mission Control centre in Houston, Texas, waited anxiously for the ship to clear the far side and re-establish contact. The mission went without a hitch and returned safely.

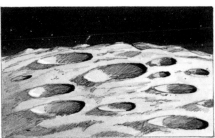

"Seas" on the Moon

Dark areas on the Moon are known as "seas". In fact they are waterless plains, formed by lava from volcanoes, now extinct (no longer active).

Struck by Meteors

The great craters which can be seen on the Moon were caused by meteors (giant rocks) crashing into the Moon's surface.

No Atmosphere

The gases of Earth's atmosphere protect us from the Sun. Without atmosphere the Moon is scorching hot by day, and freezing at night.

•DESTINATION: MOON•

The Early Apollos
The first six *Apollo* missions were designed to test von Braun's new Saturn rocket and were unmanned. In March 1969 *Apollo 9* astronauts practised docking the command ship with the lunar module in Earth's orbit.

Apollo 10
The *Apollo 10* mission was planned to test the lunar module in orbit round the Moon. Only if it was completely successful would the Moon landing go ahead. In May 1969 *Apollo 10* lifted off and headed for the Moon.

Mission badge

The three stages of the Saturn 5 *rocket* (right).

I
N 1969 *Apollo 11* was named as the craft scheduled to make the Moon landing. It consisted of three parts, or modules. The command module was nicknamed *Columbia* and would carry the astronauts for most of the journey and return with them to Earth.

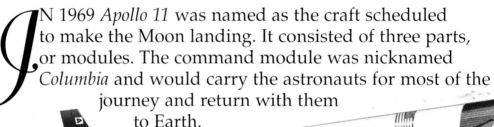

Five engines

First stage

Engines

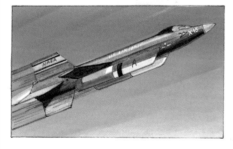

The Astronauts
Neil Armstrong
had been a pilot in the Korean War and had also test-flown rocket planes. He commanded the *Gemini 8* mission in 1966.

Buzz Aldrin
Edwin ("Buzz") Aldrin had also been a pilot in Korea. In 1966 he had piloted *Gemini 12* and walked in space for over two hours, a record time.

Michael Collins
Michael Collins had flown in *Gemini 10* in 1966. The men picked for the *Apollo 11* flight were all experienced pilots. All three were born in 1930.

•THE APOLLO 11 SPACECRAFT•

Landing Practice
As part of the test-flight two astronauts in *Apollo 10*'s lunar module descended to within 14,460 metres of the Moon's surface, but did not land. Instead they rejoined the main ship and returned to Earth.

Soviet Moon Mission
Three days before the launch of *Apollo 11*, the Soviet Union sent a spacecraft, *Luna 15*, on a mysterious Moon mission. It may have been designed to collect rock samples, but in fact it crashed on the Moon and broke up.

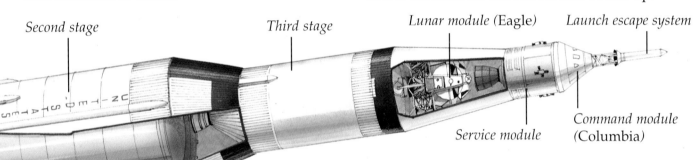

Second stage   *Third stage*   *Lunar module* (Eagle)   *Launch escape system*

Service module   *Command module (Columbia)*

Attached to *Columbia* was the service module which housed the rockets and fuel that would be needed for the round trip to the Moon. The lunar module (*Eagle*) would take two of the astronauts down to the Moon. After they had explored the surface, the *Eagle*'s rockets would fire to carry them back to *Columbia*, orbiting above.

The Apollo craft was so heavy von Braun had to design the largest rocket ever built, Saturn 5, to blast it into space. It stood 111 metres tall and was assembled at Cape Canaveral, Florida, in a building so tall that clouds sometimes gathered at the top at night. The rocket burned a mixture of kerosene and liquid oxygen.

In Training
Before the mission the three astronauts practised every move in machines called simulators which worked just like the *Apollo* craft.

Weightlessness
Once clear of Earth's gravity, all astronauts experience weightless conditions. Aldrin, Armstrong and Collins trained underwater for this.

Like Outer Space
Weightless conditions can also be experienced inside aircraft flying special curved paths. On these flights the astronauts practised moving around.

•WE HAVE LIFT-OFF!•

Early Call
The morning of 16 July dawned clear and bright. The astronauts ate a large breakfast of steak, eggs, toast, orange juice and coffee at Cape Canaveral. Then they were driven across the base to the launch pad.

On the Launch Pad
The *Saturn 5* rocket towered high above the launch pad. The astronauts were taken to the top in the launch tower lift. From the top they could see the Atlantic Ocean glinting beyond the marshland of the cape.

*L*AUNCH DAY for *Apollo 11*'s mission was 16 July 1969. Two hours before take-off the three astronauts took their seats in the command module. Buzz Aldrin, who would help fly the lunar module, sat in the centre. On Aldrin's left was Neil Armstrong, the flight commander. He would be the first to step on the Moon. On his right sat Michael Collins, the command module pilot, who would stay on board. The countdown went smoothly, and soon after 9.30am, amid a cloud of flaming gas and steam, *Apollo 11* roared into the air.

Mission Control in Houston, Texas (above).

Ready for Launch
At 9.32am *Apollo 11* was cleared for take-off. It had taken over five hours to fill the rocket's tanks with 2,000 tonnes of explosive fuel.

Ignition
As the engines ignited, a huge ball of orange flame appeared around the rocket's base. The ground shook as the rocket cleared the launch pad.

Three-Stage Rocket
The *Saturn 5* rocket had three stages. Each was jettisoned (cast away) once its fuel was used up. This lightened the load to be carried upwards.

Ready for Take-Off

Dressed in bulky spacesuits, the astronauts were helped into their seats aboard *Columbia*. Then *Columbia*'s hatch was closed. Mission Control informed the astronauts: "You are go for launch."

Audience of Millions

Thousands of spectators had gathered at a safe distance to see *Apollo 11* blast off. Millions more followed the event on television or radio, as the astronauts made their final preparations for take-off.

"Three, two, one, zero… we have lift-off!" – the excited ground crew at Cape Canaveral watched as *Apollo 11* rose into the air. The engines of the Saturn 5 rocket burned 15 tonnes of fuel per second and produced one of the loudest sounds ever heard.

Escape Tower Jettisoned

After three minutes, the launch escape tower which had fitted over the command module was jettisoned. Now the astronauts could see out.

Third Stage Ignited

Nine minutes into the flight, the second rocket stage burnt out and was jettisoned. The third stage engines took over as the rocket roared upwards.

Into Orbit

Eleven minutes after take-off, *Apollo 11* and the third stage rocket reached Earth's orbit. Final checks were made before heading for the Moon.

•ON COURSE•

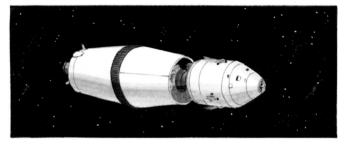

Tricky Move

Once free of Earth's orbit, command module pilot Michael Collins eased *Columbia* with the service module clear of the third stage of the *Saturn 5*. Then he turned the spacecraft around and steered back towards the rocket.

Panels Away

As *Columbia* approached, panels which had protected *Eagle* during take-off were jettisoned to reveal the flimsy craft. Not built to fly in Earth's atmosphere, the lunar module was only covered by thin layers of foil.

THREE HOURS into *Apollo 11*'s flight, Mission Control in Houston gave the astronauts permission to head for the Moon. The engines of the third stage *Saturn* rocket blasted the spacecraft free of Earth's orbit. Then, as *Apollo* hurtled towards the Moon, Michael Collins took the centre seat for a difficult manoeuvre. He had to disengage *Columbia* from the rocket and turn around to dock with the lunar module, which had been housed inside the third stage. Collins performed the delicate operation perfectly. Once *Eagle* had been retrieved, the third stage was left behind. The astronauts could settle down for their three-day journey to the Moon.

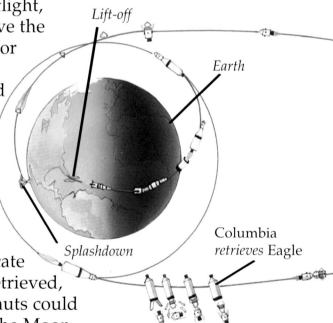

Lift-off

Earth

Splashdown

Columbia *retrieves* Eagle

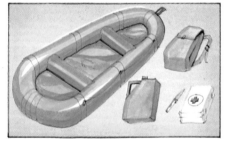

Emergency Supplies

Apollo was well stocked with supplies. Its emergency survival kit included a life raft in case the crew landed off course on Earth.

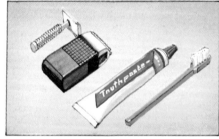

Shaving in Space

In weightless conditions, food, water and supplies had to be well packaged or they would float away. Shaving gear was adapted for zero gravity.

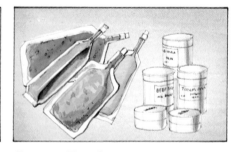

Instant Food

To save on weight, food was freeze-dried and sealed in packets. A typical meal was chicken or salmon with rice, biscuit cubes, cocoa and juice.

•APOLLO 11 LEAVES EARTH ORBIT•

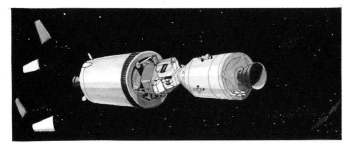

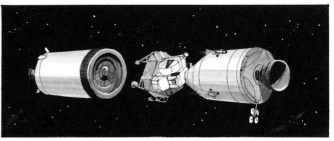

Docking

Collins manoeuvred the command module of *Apollo 11* towards *Eagle* with the help of the small rocket thrusters on the sides of the service module. Then *Columbia* docked gently with the lunar module.

Leaving Earth Behind

Collins reversed *Columbia* to disengage the lunar module from the *Saturn* rocket. Then, with *Eagle* firmly attached to the nose of the command module, *Apollo 11* headed for the Moon.

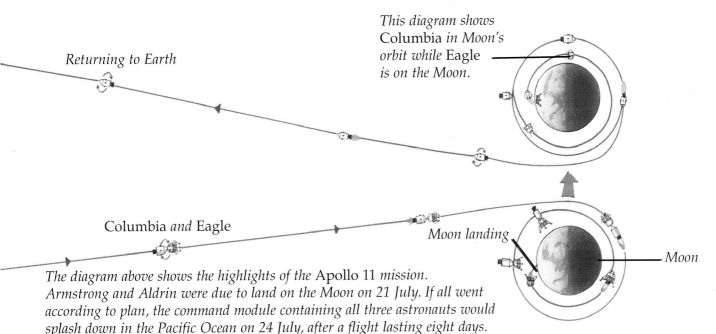

Returning to Earth

This diagram shows Columbia *in Moon's orbit while* Eagle *is on the Moon.*

Columbia *and* Eagle

Moon landing

Moon

The diagram above shows the highlights of the Apollo 11 *mission. Armstrong and Aldrin were due to land on the Moon on 21 July. If all went according to plan, the command module containing all three astronauts would splash down in the Pacific Ocean on 24 July, after a flight lasting eight days.*

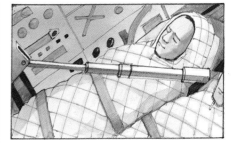

Table Manners

Hungry astronauts squirted water from a dispenser into the food packets and kneaded the bags. Then they squeezed the contents into their mouths.

Weightless Work

During the flight, a TV camera on board *Apollo 11* gave audiences on Earth a tour of the ship and showed the men working in zero gravity.

Time to Rest

During rest periods the astronauts slept in sleeping bags tied below their seats so that they would not float away across the cabin.

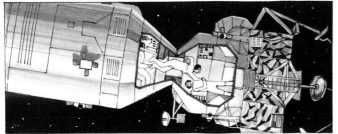

Into the Moon Lander
After breakfast on 20 July the astronauts, who had spent most of the trip in overalls, put on their spacesuits. Neil Armstrong and Buzz Aldrin floated through the connecting tunnel into *Eagle*, leaving Collins alone in *Columbia*.

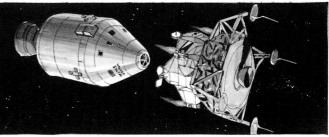

Winged Eagle
The two craft separated as they went behind the Moon again. *Columbia* continued to orbit the Moon, while *Eagle* fired its descent engine to slow down for the landing. "The Eagle has wings," Armstrong announced.

ON 19 JULY, *Apollo 11* reached the Moon. The astronauts fired *Columbia*'s rockets to enter Moon's orbit. The next day Armstrong and Aldrin moved into the lunar module, *Eagle*, leaving Collins in charge of *Columbia*. The craft separated, and *Eagle* began its descent to the Sea of Tranquillity, the landing site. Armstrong saw that the computer was about to land the craft in a crater filled with rocks. As fuel ran low he guided *Eagle* to a more level spot, and touched down gently. The promise made by President Kennedy in 1961 had been kept. Humans had landed on the Moon.

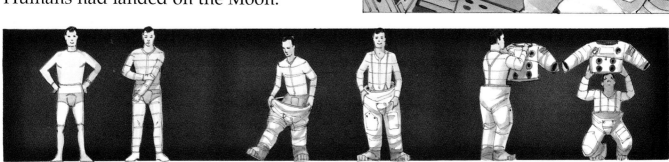

Getting Dressed
The *Apollo* astronauts wore spacesuits at critical times such as take-off and re-entry. Getting dressed was quite a lengthy process.

1. Underwear
The pressurized spacesuits were made up of several protective layers. Next to his skin each astronaut wore long underwear.

2. Extra Protection
On the Moon Armstrong and Aldrin needed extra protection from intense heat and cold. They wore special water-cooled underwear.

• APOLLO 11 LANDS ON THE MOON •

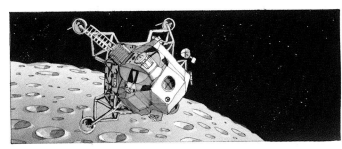

About to Land
As *Eagle* neared the surface, Armstrong spotted that they were about to land on very rough ground. If the craft tipped over, it would not be able to take off again. The two men would be stranded on the Moon.

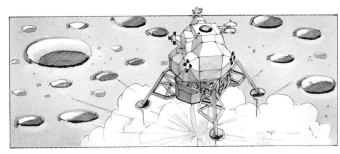

Steered to Safety
Armstrong took over control of the landing, slowed *Eagle*'s descent and steered the craft away from the crater. But the descent engine was almost out of fuel. With seconds to spare Armstrong landed safely.

During the final moments of descent, Armstrong wrestled with the controls as Aldrin called out the craft's height and speed. Fuel ran out just as one of Eagle's *feet touched the dusty ground. There was silence, and then the ground crew heard the calm voice of Neil Armstrong: "Houston, Tranquillity Base here. The* Eagle *has landed."*

3. A Practical Suit
A large pocket on the spacesuit's leg was used for collecting rock samples. They also carried backpacks with a supply of oxygen to breathe.

4. Headgear
Each astronaut wore a soft cloth helmet with a built-in microphone and earphones so he could communicate with Mission Control.

5. Finishing Touches
A hard helmet like a goldfish bowl fitted on top. Flexible over-gloves added protection on the Moon and completed the outfit.

•ONE GIANT LEAP•

Opening the Hatch
Once on the Moon, it had been planned that the astronauts would sleep for four hours before going outside. However, they were too excited to rest. The men prepared to leave, then Armstrong opened the hatch.

Walking on the Moon
On the Moon's surface, Armstrong and Aldrin practised moving around in gravity one-sixth the strength of Earth's. They tried walking, bouncing and jumping on the stony plain, but found walking worked best.

DOWN AT Tranquillity Base, Armstrong and Aldrin got into their life-support units and the protective clothing they would need. Armstrong opened *Eagle*'s hatch, then stepped down onto the surface of the Moon. "That's one small step for a man, one giant leap for mankind," he said. Buzz Aldrin joined him, and the two astronauts planted the American flag. They listened to their radios as Richard Nixon, the new American president, congratulated them on the success of one of the greatest achievements of all time.

Armstrong jumped down onto the Moon.

Moonrock
The astronauts collected 22 kilograms of rocks and soil. The rocks turned out to be similar to those on Earth, but much older.

Precious Dust
When magnified, Moon dust collected from the Sea of Tranquillity was found to contain tiny pieces of glass that shine like jewels.

Left on the Moon
Footprints left on the Moon by Armstrong and Aldrin will last for thousands of years. There is no wind or rain to blow or wash them away.

•HUMAN BEINGS WALK ON THE MOON•

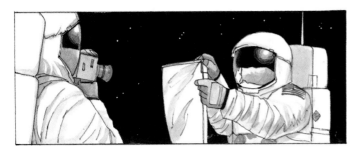

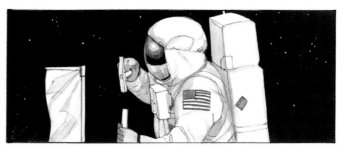

Scientific Mission
NASA scientists had given the astronauts a number of tasks to carry out on the Moon. As Armstrong filmed, Aldrin set up a metal foil strip which was used to take scientific measurements.

Taking Samples
Aldrin hammered a hollow tube into the ground to collect a sample of Moon soil which would be analyzed by scientists back on Earth. He also set up an instrument designed to measure "Moonquakes".

The astronauts spent two-and-a-half hours on the lunar surface. They set up many experiments, including a laser mirror which was used by scientists to measure the exact distance between the Earth and the Moon.

Flying the Flag
The flag planted by the astronauts was held out straight by a metal rod along the top, because there is no wind to make the flag flutter.

Medals for Space Heroes
The astronauts also left medals and badges on the Moon in memory of all those who had died during the history of space travel.

Making History
During the Moon trip Neil Armstrong uncovered a metal plaque to mark the first Moon visit. It reads "We came in peace for all mankind."

•MISSION ACCOMPLISHED•

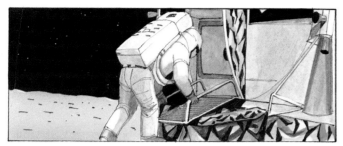

Last to Leave

When the astronauts had completed their tasks, they returned to *Eagle*. Armstrong was the last to leave. He climbed the ladder and squeezed through the hatch. Then the hatch was closed.

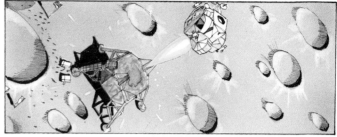

Take-Off from the Moon

Eagle's ascent rocket was the only part of the *Apollo 11* spacecraft which had no back-up system. But it fired smoothly and the little craft soared upwards towards *Columbia*, which was orbiting above to take the astronauts home.

BACK IN THE lunar module, the astronauts prepared for take-off. Aldrin fired *Eagle*'s ascent engine anxiously. If the rocket failed they would be trapped on the Moon. But all was well, and *Eagle* blasted upwards to meet *Columbia*. Reunited, the three astronauts returned to Earth in *Columbia* and splashed down safely in the Ocean. They were immediately placed in isolation, or quarantine, in case they had brought back any dangerous Moon germs. But doctors soon declared that they were all perfectly healthy.

While Armstrong and Aldrin were on the Moon Collins orbited above in Columbia. He was glad see his fellow astronauts when they returned.

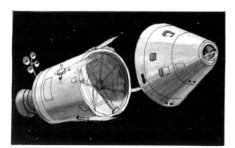

Return Trip

Apollo 11 approached the Earth at a speed of 27,000 kilometres per hour. *Columbia* then separated from the service module.

Re-Entry into the Atmosphere

Columbia was coated with a special layer to withstand the heat of re-entry. The layer burned, but inside the astronauts were safe.

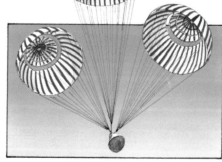

Parachutes Open

As command module *Columbia* dropped through the air, large parachutes stored in the nose-cone opened to slow the spacecraft's fall.

• APOLLO 11 RETURNS TO EARTH •

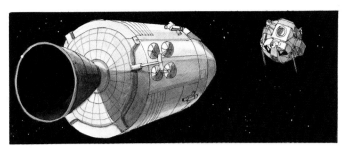

The Lonely Astronaut
Alone in *Columbia* round the far side of the Moon, Collins was out of contact with Earth and the other astronauts. A newspaper called him "the loneliest man in the universe". He watched eagerly as *Eagle* approached.

Reunited
The two craft docked successfully. Then Collins opened the connecting hatch, and Armstrong and Aldrin floated through to join him. *Eagle* was abandoned as the command module, *Columbia* , headed back to Earth.

In an isolation container on board the recovery ship, the astronauts were greeted by President Nixon. After 20 days doctors declared the astronauts fit and healthy. When their quarantine ended, they were driven through the streets of America, and cheered as heroes. They went on to tour many countries and received a heroes' welcome wherever they went.

Splashdown
Columbia splashed down in the Pacific Ocean and then turned upside down. Balloons released from the nose-cone turned it the right way up.

Helicopter Rescue
As *Columbia* bobbed in the ocean, crew from the US navy ship *Hornet* arrived in a helicopter to rescue the astronauts.

Lifted to Safety
The men were winched up into the helicopter and flown to the *Hornet*, where they entered the isolation container for their quarantine.

Unlucky 13

Two days into the *Apollo 13* mission, an explosion badly damaged the command module's life-support system. The Moon landing was abandoned and the crew only just made it safely back to Earth.

SIX OTHER *Apollo* missions were launched after *Apollo 11*. Five were successful, but *Apollo 13* was nearly a disaster. About 330,000 kilometres from Earth, an explosion on board damaged the craft. The crew had to rely on supplies of power, water and breathable air from their lunar module as they looped around the Moon and headed back to Earth. They splashed down safely. The other five *Apollo* missions landed on the Moon. Meanwhile the Soviet Union had concentrated on putting space stations in Earth orbit, and sending probes without cosmonauts to explore space.

The Last Apollos

In 1972, *Apollo 17* was the last mission with a crew to be sent to the Moon. Astronauts Eugene Cernan and Harrison Schmitt spent 22 hours on the Moon's surface.

In 1975 a Soviet Soyuz *craft docked with an American* Apollo *in space. The crews visited each other.*

Living in Space

Astronauts spending long periods on board space stations must exercise every day or their muscles will begin to weaken.

Taking a Bath

In zero gravity bathing is difficult, because the water tends to float away! Special showers help astronauts to keep clean in space.

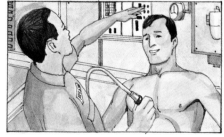

Staying Healthy

Astronauts in space for long periods can develop health problems connected with being weightless. Medical checks make sure they are fit.

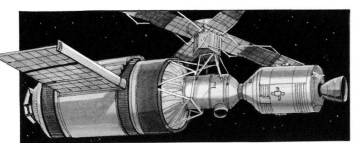

Space Stations
When the *Apollo* missions ended America concentrated on building a space station. *Skylab* was launched in 1974 but only operated for six months.

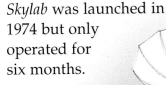

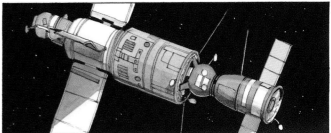

Soviet Skill
By the early 1970s the Soviet Union had gained more experience than the Americans in operating space stations. In 1974 cosmonauts spent a record 63 days in the space station *Salyut 4*.

On the later Apollo missions astronauts travelled on the Moon's surface in buggies called lunar roving vehicles. These were battery-powered and carried astronauts up to six kilometres from the lunar module to explore and carry out experiments.

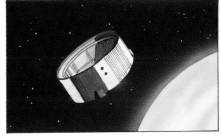

Dangers of Space
Spacecraft orbiting high above the Earth risk being struck by showers of meteoroids. A strong double outer layer provides them with protection.

Sunscreen
Out in space it is unbearably hot in the Sun's glare, and freezing cold in the shadows. The *Skylab* crew had to rig a sunshade to protect the craft.

Space Litter
After years of space exploration, there are many dead satellites in orbit round the Earth. Spacecraft must be careful to avoid collisions!

THE UNITED STATES spent enormous sums of money on the *Apollo* project. By the time the *Apollo 17* astronauts left the Moon, the project had cost a staggering $25 billion. Each expensive Apollo craft was only used once, then thrown away. In the 1980s and 1990s, both America and the Soviet Union developed reusable spacecraft, built to fly a series of missions, not just one. The Soviet Union has led in the development of space stations, and both countries have sent probes to other planets in our solar system. In recent years other countries, including China, Japan and Europe, have also begun their own space programmes.

THE SPACE SHUTTLE is America's reusable spacecraft. It was first launched in 1981. It launches like a rocket, with the aid of strap-on booster rockets and a large main fuel tank, which is jettisoned soon after take-off.

WHAT HAPPENED NEXT?

The shuttle carries new satellites into orbit. It may also carry up to seven astronauts on board. They may leave the craft in spacesuits to repair satellites and other space equipment. Outside the craft, astronauts move around using a Manned Manoeuvring Unit (MMU), a pack containing a life-support system and gas jets for moving around.

In 1992 American astronauts spent eight hours in space repairing the communications satellite *Intelsat 6*. When the shuttle's tasks are done, it returns to Earth and lands on a runway, like an aeroplane. Within two weeks it may be ready for another mission. The shuttle project has been mostly successful, although it had a major setback in 1986. Just after lift-off, the shuttle *Challenger* caught fire and exploded, killing all seven crew. After this disaster, the project was re-examined carefully to find out what had gone wrong and to make sure it never happened again.

AFTER SUCCESS with early prototype space stations, the Soviet Union launched space station *Mir* in 1986. Since then *Mir* has been occupied continuously by different crews who spend months in space doing research. Soviet cosmonauts have set the records for the longest periods spent in space. Yuri Romanenko spent over a year in space, on three separate missions.

SINCE THE 1970s probes without crews have revealed many of the secrets of our solar system. The American probe *Mariner 2* was first to visit another planet, Venus, in 1962. *Mariner 9* orbited Mars. *Voyagers 1* and *2* were launched in 1977. They visited Jupiter, Saturn and Uranus and then left the solar system. They are still sending back signals. The Hubble space telescope was launched in 1990 and repaired by astronauts in 1993. Orbiting high above the Earth, this powerful, giant telescope sends back the clearest pictures yet of distant stars out in deep space.

•GLOSSARY•

Altitude
Height, usually above sea level.

Atmosphere
A layer of gases, including oxygen, surrounding the Earth.

Booster
A rocket engine strapped to a spacecraft which gives a short burst of extra power, particularly during take-off.

Cosmonaut
The Russian word for astronaut.

Docking
The linking of two craft in space.

G force
A measure of the force of gravity.

Jettison
To release or throw away.

Liquid fuel
A fuel normally in gas form, but which has been made into liquid through extreme cooling.

Lunar
Relating to the Moon.

Manoeuvre
A planned movement, or to move.

Module
A section of a spacecraft.

Orbit
The curved path of one object circling another.

Probe
A small craft not built to carry human passengers.

Prototype
An original model.

Simulator
A machine built to imitate the conditions of another environment.

Splashdown
A sea-landing after a space flight.

Stage
A section of a rocket.

Thrust
The pushing power produced by a rocket's engine.

Thruster
A small rocket motor used by a spacecraft to manoeuvre.

Zero gravity
The condition of weightlessness that exists beyond the pull of gravity.

Quarantine
A period passed in isolation, for health reasons.

Re-entry
The return of a spacecraft to Earth's atmosphere.

Satellite
An object circling a larger body in space, such as a planet. The Moon is a satellite of the Earth.

INDEX